CONTENTS

820

KU-481-910

*subject to availability

How to use this book

This book is designed to support your study of the OCR poetry and short story collections – **Opening Lines** and **Opening Worlds**. It will help you to enjoy and explore the poems and stories and prepare you for writing about them in your exams and in your coursework folders. The book is written for you as an individual student and it is possible to work through it on your own. However, it is likely to be a more helpful experience if you use it in a group or class context, alongside your teachers and fellow-students. The book provides:

- an outline of how the collections fit into your course
- guidance on the Assessment Objectives and what the examiners are looking for
- general introductions to the study of poetry and short stories
- activities to help you explore the poetry sections and the stories in detail
- strategies for linking, pairing and comparing poems and stories
- sample exam questions and coursework ideas
- extracts from sample answers with examiner comments
- advice on using quotations and on structuring comparisons
- suggestions for further study in extension panels
- background information on the writers
- a glossary explaining all the technical terms used, and italicised, in the book.

We hope that the book will help you to enjoy some wonderful stories and poems, and to achieve exam success as well.

How the collections fit into your courses

The two collections are remarkably versatile and can be used in a number of different ways in each of your English courses. It all depends on your choices and particularly on which English Literature course you choose to follow (for Scheme A use Units 1–4 **or** for Scheme B use Units 5–8) but it's possible for you to cover **60%** of your English Literature course and **15%** of your English course with work based on these two texts alone.

OPENING LINES (poetry)	OPENING WORLDS (short stories)
English: Coursework, Unit 4 Literary Heritage = 5% (or Exam, Unit 3 Literary Heritage = 5%)	**English:** Exam, Unit 2 Different Cultures = 10%
English Literature: Exam, Unit 2 or 5 Poetry = 25% Coursework, Unit 3 or 7 Prose = 10% (or Exam, Unit 4 or 8 Prose =10%)	**English Literature:** Exam, Unit 2 Prose = 25% Coursework, Unit 7 Prose = 10% (or Exam, Unit 8 Prose = 10%)

820

Working with
OPENING WORLDS
& OPENING LINES

Michele Paule

Steve Cooper and Anna Gregory (Experienced examiners)

www.heinemann.co.uk
✓ Free online support
✓ Useful weblinks
✓ 24 hour online ordering

01865 888058

Heinemann Educational Publishers
Halley Court, Jordan Hill, Oxford OX2 8EJ
Part of Harcourt Education

Heinemann is the registered trademark of
Harcourt Education Limited

First published 2002
Second edition published 2004

09 08 07
10 9 8 7 6 5 4

British Library Cataloguing in Publication Data is available from the British Library on request.

13-digit ISBN: 978 0 435150 93 8

Designed and produced by 320 Design

Cover design by hicksdesign

Cover photographs: Getty Images (inset); Hulton Archive (background)

Original illustrations © Harcourt Education Limited, 2002
Illustrated by John Holder, pp. 25, 32, 81; David Hopkins, pp. 30, 37, 43, 46, 61, 80, 86, 97, 98, 104, 116, 125; Rachael Wilkinson, p. 123.

Printed in the UK by Scotprint

The publishers would like to thank the following for permission to reproduce photographs on the pages noted: Art and Culture Magazine, Matichon Group, Thailand, p.150; Camera Press, pp.144, 171, 177; Camera Press/Jane Bown, p.165; Camera Press/Miriam Berkley, p.141; Camera Press/John Reardon, p.147; Corbis/Reuters NewMedia Inc, p.153; ″ 2000 Enorth.co.cn, Tianjin Enorth Co Ltd, p.156; Peepal Tree Press, p.162; Shiel Land Associates, p.168; Trevor Sealy, p.159.

English

You have to write about poetry as part of the reading requirement for your coursework (Unit 4) or for the exam alternative to coursework (Unit 3). You can choose to use any of the Post-1914 poets (or the Pre-1914 poets marked NC) in **Opening Lines** for coursework. You can choose to study **Opening Worlds** as your prose text for the *Different Cultures* exam (Unit 2) and only half of the stories (six in total) will be set for this exam.

English Literature

In **Scheme A**, 70% of your marks will come from exam work on Post-1914 texts and 30% from coursework on Pre-1914 texts. You can choose to study one of the Post-1914 Sections in **Opening Lines** as your poetry text for the exam and the twelve stories in **Opening Worlds** as your prose text. You can also use some Pre-1914 poems from **Opening Lines** for your coursework (or for the exam alternative to coursework).

In **Scheme B**, 70% of your marks will come from exam work on Pre-1914 texts and 30% for coursework on Post-1914 texts. You can choose a Pre-1914 Section from **Opening Lines** as your poetry text for the exam and use some of its Post-1914 poems for your coursework (or for the exam alternative to coursework). Because the **Opening Worlds** stories are all Post-1914, you can only use them for coursework (or for the exam alternative to coursework) in Scheme B.

Making sense of the Assessment Objectives

The Assessment Objectives sum up what you have to do to succeed in English and English Literature. The examiners will keep these in mind as they mark your work.

English Literature

Your work on the two collections will help you to achieve all of the Assessment Objectives for English Literature, which are as follows:

1 **Respond to texts critically, sensitively and in detail, selecting appropriate ways to convey your response, using textual evidence as appropriate.** Show that you know your texts well, that you have thought about them and you can support your ideas and insights with direct quotation and other textual references. You can also express your responses to the texts in a clear, organised and detailed way.

2 **Explore how language, structure and forms contribute to the meaning of texts, considering different approaches to texts and alternative interpretations.** Show awareness of the way in which a text is written rather than just concentrating on content (the '**how** is it written' rather than '**what** is it about' approach). This awareness of the choices that a writer makes to convey a range of meanings and to achieve a range of effects is a key element in achieving high marks.

3 **Explore relationships between texts, selecting and evaluating relevant material.** Show that you can compare texts, looking closely at links/contrasts, similarities/differences. Your work on pairs of poems from **Opening Lines** could be central to achieving this objective, both in your exams and your coursework.

4 **Relate texts to their social, cultural and historical contexts and literary traditions.** All the exam questions on **Opening Worlds** and other prose texts will enable you to show awareness of the context which frames a particular story or novel. The questions may invite you to explore the presentation of particular attitudes and beliefs in the texts, for instance, or to focus on the reasons for social or personal conflict. The *contextual,* like the *comparative,* requirement is a compulsory element for your exams and your coursework, and the twelve stories in **Opening Worlds**, which depict a wide range of cultures, could be central to achieving this objective.

English

Your work on the two collections will also help you to achieve two of the key Assessment Objectives for English. These objectives are very similar to Objectives 1 and 2 for English Literature.

1 **Read with insight and engagement, making appropriate references to text and developing and sustaining interpretations of them.**

2 **Understand and evaluate how writers use linguistic, structural and presentational devices to achieve their effects, and comment on ways language changes and varies.**

Annotation

From June 2005 there is a rule change for the examination. You will not be allowed to write notes in the texts which you take with you into the exams. A lot of notes written in the margin can sometimes stop you from expressing your own ideas or distract you from answering the question directly. So, for the exams from June 2005 onwards, you will be supplied with working copies of both **Opening Lines** and **Opening Worlds**, which you can annotate as you wish throughout the course, and then with clean copies for use in the exams.

OPENING LINES

poetry past and present

2003–2008

Skills

OPENING LINES

First reading

Your first reading of a poem will give you an overview. To understand a poem in more depth and detail you will need to re-read it more than once. However, the first time you read any poem you should be able to identify a few important things.

The poems in **Opening Lines** have been grouped together into sections, such as 'Men and Women' and 'Town and Country', because they focus on similar subjects. So, your first clues to what the poem may be about come in the section heading. For example, poems in the section entitled 'Generations' will be about parents and children and the differences between the elderly and the young.

As you read a poem for the first time, ask yourself the following questions:

What is the poem about?

- Does it describe a place or a person?
- Is it a remembered event?
- Is it a subject the poet feels strongly about?

What (if anything) happens in the poem?

- Does it tell a story?
- Does it describe an important moment in time? If so, what happens?

Is it about a thing or a place?

- Does it describe a setting in detail?
- Where does it seem to be?
- Why is it important?

What are the main feelings/moods in the poem?

- What is the poet's attitude to the subject?
- What emotions are suggested? Anger? Fear? Sorrow? Love? Lust? Fun?

Who (if anyone) is the poem to or from?

- Does it seem to be to a particular person? E.g. parent/child/lover?
- Does it seem to be a personal poem?
- Is it written to show a larger, more general group of readers a particular view of something?

! Remember

It is a good idea to make a note of any words you don't understand in the poem you are reading.

- Make a note of what the word might mean in the context of the poem as a whole. Are there any clues?
- Discuss the word with a partner.
- Then check with a teacher or refer to a dictionary.

Sharing your findings

1 Get into groups. Each member of the group should choose a different poem to read from the section you are studying.

2 When you have read your poem, copy and complete the chart below.

3 Share your results with your group to create one large chart for a range of the poems.

Title & poet	Subject	To/from	Events	Mood/feelings

4 When your group has completed their table, share your results with another group, until you have a good range of the poems.

Creating a concept map

Staying in your groups, work through the following steps to create a concept map or image, using the example from Section F: **The 1914–18 War [i]** below as your model.

1 On a large piece of paper, write all the poem titles in the section you are studying. Make sure they are evenly spaced.

2 Next, try to think of connections between pairs of poems. When you have thought of a connection, draw a line between the two poem titles.

3 Along the line you have drawn, briefly describe what the connection is.

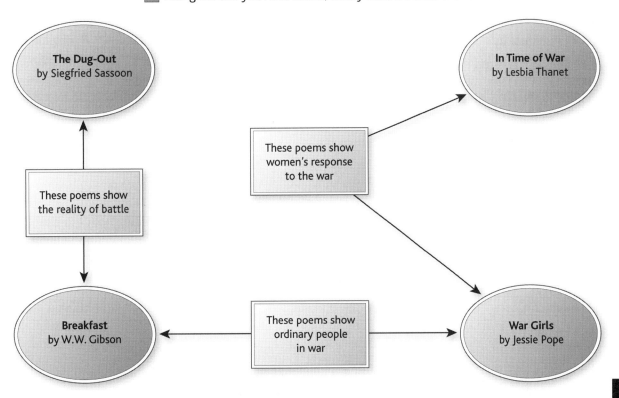

Imagery

Imagery in poetry consists of the pictures the words create in the mind of the reader. Some of the ways in which poets create images include:

- sound – rhyme, rhythm, onomatopoiea, assonance
- vivid description
- association of ideas
- use of *symbols* that have a wider meaning
- use of *similes* and *metaphors*.

Look at the examples in the chart below, which are all taken from poems in **Opening Lines**. Copy and complete the chart.

How are the images created? What do they suggest to you?

Image	Suggested idea
The long yawn of Infancy	metaphor suggesting babyhood is boring
Dawn breaks open like a wound that bleeds afresh	simile that links the red sky to a bleeding wound, suggesting the new day will be as violent as the day before
All I ever did was follow in his tall shadow	
When, his pulse failing, Passion speechless lies	
The little window where the sun Came peeping in at morn	
The rain is full of ghosts tonight, that tap and sigh, upon the glass and listen	
The merciless east winds that knive us	
Dad kept her slippers warming	
Life storms through you	

A poet will often use a range of similar images to build up a picture. It is useful to see if there is a pattern in a poem that you can comment on.

Extension

In the poem **Long Distance**, from the 'Generations' section, the poet builds up a series of images of everyday domestic routines that show the father taking care of his wife, and how he cannot let go.

- Find some of these domestic images in the poem to support this statement.

- See if you can identify a range of related images in another poem from the section you are studying.

Looking at language

Exploring the language of poetry can mean you have a whole range of things to look at, from *metaphors* and *similes* to sounds and *dialects*. Because poems are usually shorter than plays or novels, the language in them is often more carefully chosen and more intense. A poet has less space to convey important experiences, feelings or ideas, so the words he or she chooses have to work harder.

In the poems in this collection, you will see poets using language in a variety of ways to achieve particular effects.

The Glossary (on pages 188–91) explains some of the language features and their effects, with examples from poems in the **Collection**. You don't need to use the technical terms in order to understand and explain poetry, but they will help you to express your ideas more clearly.

Experts use technical language to make their jobs easier. For example, learning the names of engine parts doesn't tell you how to fix a car, but it helps mechanics to describe what is going on. So, in a garage, it makes more sense to say 'I think the carburettor is faulty' **than** 'I think we need to fix the bit that mixes the air with the petrol so that the engine can burn it properly.'

Words that do the work

Looking at language in poetry could also be described as finding the words that do the work – and then explaining the work they do. Thinking of poetry in this way will help you to:

- read the poem and judge its effects on you by picking out key words and phrases that make an impression
- use examples and quotations from poems to support the ideas you have
- follow up your points and quotations with explanations/analysis of language.

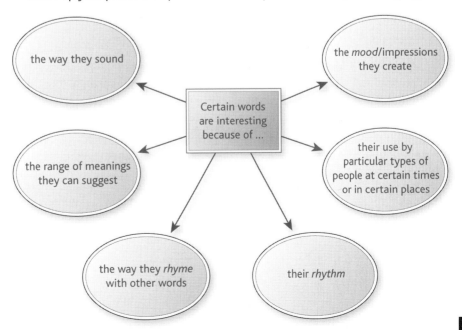

the way they sound

the *mood*/impressions they create

Certain words are interesting because of …

the range of meanings they can suggest

their use by particular types of people at certain times or in certain places

the way they *rhyme* with other words

their *rhythm*

Developing your exploration of language

Look at the section of **Opening Lines** you are studying and work through some of these activities, *either* on the same poem, *or* choose a different poem for each one.

Sound

1
Choose a poem.
- Underline the words the poet has used for their sound as well as their meaning.
- Use the Glossary to identify the technique.
- Think about why sound is important here and what it adds to the poem.

Rhyme

2
Find a poem which makes use of rhyme and make a note of rhyming pairs of words.
- Do they reinforce each other?
- Do they contrast?

Dialect/colloquialism

3
Find a poem which makes use of less formal or colloquial language.
- Is this language used throughout or only occasionally?
- Why do you think the poet has used this language?
- Is s/he trying to suggest something in particular?
- Is s/he trying to convey an idea of character? Setting? Time?

Mood

4
Choose a poem that seems on first reading to have a strong sense of mood.
- Read it through again and highlight/make a note of the words and phrases that seem to you to help create the mood.
- Explain how each word or phrase helps to create the mood.

General

5
- Underline/highlight/make a note of words that you think are interesting.
- Using the suggestions above and the Glossary, try to explain what 'work' these words are doing in the poem.

As a class/in groups

6
For the section you are studying, create your own chart for looking at language, identifying some language features and then describing the effect they have.

Structure

The *structure* of a poem is the way it is constructed or arranged as a whole. Poets use structure to help organise their stories or ideas, to help create flow or rhythm, or sometimes to follow a tradition.

Thinking about the structure of a poem can be important because:

- it helps you to understand how the mood, feeling or ideas in the poem are being suggested to you
- it shows that you are aware that you are writing about poetry rather than stories or prose.

When writing about structure, as when writing about language, the rule is to think about the effect on you as a reader – and to explain it.

As with poetic language, there are some key terms and features you should be familiar with when you are reading and writing about structure. The Glossary (on pages 188–91) will help you to become familiar with these technical terms, and suggests some ways in which structure can help convey mood and meaning.

When looking at the structure of the poem, ask yourself the following questions:

Is the poem divided into stanzas? *If so, do they:*

- tell the stages of a story?
- structure an argument?
- show different views of a subject?
- show changes in the speaker?
- show the stages of the poet's thinking?
- show the passage of time?

Is there a noticeable rhythm/metre? *If so, does it:*

- reflect the mood or subject?
- change according to mood or subject?

Is the poem structured in a traditional form, e.g. sonnet, ballad? *If so, does it:*

- have a traditional form?
- contrast form and meaning?
- follow the rules exactly?
- break the rules?

Exploring and understanding structure

1 In pairs, choose a poem each from the section you are studying but one that you have not studied before, which is structured in clear *stanzas*.

   a Write it out in your exercise book or word-process it as continuous prose. What difference does this make to the structure?

   b Exchange poems with your partner and try to organise your partner's poem back into lines/stanzas, making a note of the reasons for your choices.

   c Then compare your version with the original. Why do you think the poet structured the original as s/he has?

2 Now, each choose a poem that makes use of *punctuation*, and with sentences that do not necessarily start or finish at the ends of the lines.

   a Copy out the poem without the punctuation.

   b Exchange poems with your partner and punctuate your partner's poem, thinking about where it is important to create pauses and where it is important to maintain the flow.

   c Compare your poem with the original, thinking about why/how the poet has used punctuation.

3 In pairs, choose two poems from the section you are studying.

   a Working on one poem each, identify some key features of the structure. Explain to your partner how those features work and what they add to the poem.

   b Make notes of your own and your partner's ideas.

   c Join another pair and discuss your ideas.

◎ Extension

Using the school library or the Internet:

- find out about different *metres* and note down examples of their use

- find out about three traditional *forms* of poetry and note down examples. What sort of poems are they usually used for?

Exploring your own response

Evaluation means judging the poem, deciding which parts you thought were effective and offering a personal response. This shows you have formed opinions about what you are reading, and are not just recycling class notes.

You usually offer your own response at the end of a piece of writing, although you can make evaluative remarks throughout such as those on the left.

A successful response goes beyond just saying whether you like a poem or not. When you evaluate, you should look at the poem as a whole, and say whether you think the various elements work together well, and how clearly you think the poet has suggested key ideas or feelings. You can also say whether you agree or disagree with the ideas expressed, and describe any strong feelings that the poem produced in you.

To practise responding to poems you have studied, use some of the following ideas:

1 Brainstorm/concept-map the key features of the poem to help you gain an overview of how they work together.

2 With a partner, generate statements about poems for each other to justify, e.g. This poem creates a strong sense of place; this poem is very nostalgic.

3 Have a poetry balloon debate. Each person in the balloon has to justify why their chosen poem should not be thrown out.

4 Create poetry 'Oscars'. Decide the categories, e.g. 'most vivid ideas of horror of war', 'most interesting use of rhythm', 'strongest sense of place'. Write a brief acceptance speech for the winning poems in each category, explaining what you think the strengths are.

Remember

When exploring your own response, include a range of the features of the poem you have studied such as language, imagery, structure.

Comparing poems

When you compare things, it is often more interesting and useful to compare what is different about them than what is similar.

If you were asked to compare a cat and a killer whale and you focused on the similarities, you wouldn't find out much about either. Your list of points would probably look something like this:

- both mammals
- both like to eat fish
- both predators
- both often kept for the amusement of people.

Try focusing on the differences and see how much more detail you can produce.

1 Copy and complete the chart below.

Cats	Killer whales
Live on land	Live in the sea
Have fur	
	Have fins

The poems in **Opening Lines** are grouped together in sections which deal with similar themes and ideas. However, what makes them special as poems are the different techniques the poets have used. By focusing on the differences you can show a much more detailed understanding of how poetry works, and this is what gains marks in exams and coursework.

! Remember

When writing a comparative essay, deal with similarities in the subject first, and then focus on differences in poetic features.

2 Create a chart of similarities and differences for two poems from the section you are studying to test this theory, based on the example below.

Composed Upon Westminster Bridge . . .	London
Sonnet	
	Political

Poetry for examination in 2003–2006

Men and Women

OPENING LINES

The poems in this section focus on a theme which is as interesting today as it was when the poems were written – the relationships between men and women. Some of the poems are very much influenced by the times in which they were written, others suggest views and feelings that apply equally well today.

1 Before reading the poems, discuss these statements with a partner. Do you agree or disagree with each statement? Give reasons for your views.

a Women are fickle.

b Attitudes to men and women's love lives are different.

c It is hard to find ways to express true love.

d You believe your lover even when it is clear he/she is lying.

e Men always chase younger faces.

f Women are more constant than men.

g Men are faithful.

h Breaking up is hard to do.

i Marriage is a trap for women more than for men.

j Men do the seducing; women are seduced.

k When you are in love you live in your own little world.

l When you are rejected, you have to pretend you don't care.

Then and now

In the film *Pretty Woman*, attitudes towards men and women's love lives are different.
The song 'Tears of a clown' shows someone pretending they don't care about breaking up.

2 When you have discussed the statements, try to think of a modern song, poem or film that takes the same view for each one. Look at the example on the left:

a Are some difficult to match? What might this suggest about changing attitudes?

b Which, if any, of the attitudes have changed in modern times?

Group activity

3 Work in a group. Each student should take 3–4 poems and decide which of the above statements applies to each poem. Share your findings with the rest of your group.

a Do some of the poems seem to express more than one statement?

b Are some of the ideas in the statements more true of some poems than others?

Comparing poems

4 Choose two poems that seem to express the same idea. Use the 'Comparing poems' section on page 16 to help you explore the similarities and differences.

To His Coy Mistress Andrew Marvell

Content and theme

1. Who is this poem addressed to and who is it from?

2. What does 'coy' mean here? What is he trying to persuade the woman to do?

Structure

3. This poem is written in the form of a continuous argument. How does the poet use *punctuation* and *enjambment* to sustain the flow?

4. The poem has pace and *rhythm*. Why does the poet build momentum?

5. When you look closely at the argument, you can see it is divided into three stages. Summarise the three stages of the argument by completing these descriptions.

Stage 1	Stage 2	Stage 3
If we had lots of time I could . . .	But we can't wait too long because . . .	So what we should do is . . .

Imagery

6. The poet uses some vivid images to make his argument more convincing. Find examples of *images* suggesting the following ideas. Explain how each one works:

  • slow passage of time   • death and decay   • passion.

Language

7. Match the quotation to the relevant technique in a table like the one below and explain how each technique works. Then look for more examples of each technique.

Technique	Quotation
Exaggerated praise	'Youthful hue'/'morning dew'
Flattery	'dust'/'lust'
Mockery	'An hundred years should go to praise/Thine eyes'
Rhyme which reinforces meaning	'you deserve this state'
Rhyme which contrasts	'your quaint honour'

Exploring your own response

8. Try to justify the following statements about the poem.

  a The *structure* and *imagery* in this poem suggest a passionate and impatient man.
  b The speaker is a bully, trying to ridicule and frighten a woman into having sex.
  c The speaker uses a range of clever techniques with humour to get his own way.

The Ruined Maid Thomas Hardy

Content and theme

In Hardy's time, a woman who had sexual experience before marriage or became a mistress was considered 'ruined'. This meant she was cast out by society, to a life of prostitution or poverty.

1 The poem creates a *dialogue* between two women. What is their position and in what circumstances is the conversation taking place?

Language

The poem uses *colloquial* language to suggest the social position and background of the two women.

2 Find examples which suggest that they are uneducated and/or country girls. Why is it important that Hardy uses such language?

3 The main speaker uses some dramatic words and images whereas 'Melia's replies seem more practical. Find examples from each speaker that show this.

4 What is Hardy suggesting about the warnings girls get compared with the reality of life for 'ruined' women?

Imagery

5 **The Ruined Maid** contains *images* that contrast 'Melia's life before she was 'ruined' and after. Copy and complete the chart below with all the images you can find. Explain how the contrasts work to show the actual differences in her lifestyle.

Before	After	Explanation
in tatters, without shoes or socks	gay bracelets and bright feathers three	she used to wear rags but now has flashy clothes and jewellery
thee/thou etc		
	We never do work	

Structure

6 The poem is written in six *stanzas*. Summarise the aspect of life each stanza describes e.g. clothes, work, accent.

7 Each stanza is formed of three lines from the main speaker, followed by one line of 'Melia's response. How does this help create *rhythm*? And humour?

8 How does the last line reverse what would be the usual social position of the women? Who is patronising who?

Exploring your own response

9 This is a comic poem. How has Hardy achieved humour through challenging expectations?

10 The poem could also be said to have a serious message. Try to justify these statements:

a Hardy shows how the harshness of their lives tempts girls to stray.

b Hardy suggests that a desire for superficial finery tempts girls to 'ruin'.

A Woman Is a Worthy Thing Anon
and Upon Julia's Clothes Robert Herrick

Content and theme

1. Both these poems offer further but different views of women. What is it about women that each poet finds appealing?

Imagery

2. Both poets use very different *imagery* to build two very different views. **Upon Julia's Clothes** offers a sensual and seductive picture; **A Woman ...** creates a vision of women that is both holy and domestic. Look at the images from each poem in the table below and discuss what image of women is created.

A Woman is a Worthy Thing	Upon Julia's Clothes
• light as any roe • Our blessed lady • do the wash and do the wring • she doth thee sing/And yet she hath but care and wo • serveth a man both day and night	• in silks • sweetly flows • liquefaction of her clothes • brave vibration • that glittering taketh me

Language

3. These poems contain some words and sentence structures we no longer use in everyday speech. Identify them, find out their meaning and give their modern equivalent.

Structure

4. Look at the structuring of the poems into *stanzas*. Can you work out why each poem is organised in the way it is?

5. Both these poems have a regular *rhythm* and *rhyme scheme*. Work out the rhyme pattern for each by marking the rhyming words at the ends of lines, e.g. 'see'/'free'/'me'. Colour-code the different rhymes and see if any are repeated and how often.

6. Look at and comment on the way the rhymed words work together.

7. How does the rhythm of each poem fit the subject?

Exploring your own response

8. Compare the view of women in each poem and the ways it is presented.

9. Do similar views of women exist in modern literary and media texts? Is there a wider range of attitudes today?

Since there's no help . . . Michael Drayton

Content and theme

1 Read through the poem and answer the following questions.

    a What is the situation of the speaker?
    b Who is the poem to?
    c What feelings is he describing?
    d Is he being honest?

Imagery

2 Think about this image: 'Shake hands for ever'. How does this suggest:

- the break-up is mutual
- the break-up is final?

3 The poem contains an *extended metaphor* or image of the end of love as a death-bed scene. Note down the ways in which this scene is created using:

- *personification* of feelings as characters in the scene
- description of a physical death.

4 How does the image in the final two lines continue the death-bed analogy and contradict the images you have just explored?

Language

5 What is suggested by 'you get no more of me'?

6 Why do you think the poet repeats the word 'glad' ?

7 Highlight all the negative words you can find in the first half of the poem. What effect is created by them?

8 Look at the use of *rhyme*. Find examples where rhyme is used to:

- contrast meaning, e.g. 'heart'/'part'
- reinforce meaning, e.g. 'me'/'free'.

Why are these important in a poem in which feelings are strong and the poet is not honest about his feelings?

Structure

9 This poem is a *sonnet*. In what ways does it conform to a traditional sonnet?

10 Trace the development of the poet's feelings as the poem progresses. Note the changes in a flow chart, as below.

Denial/gladness → Death/mourning → Hope/vulnerability

11 Why do you think the last two lines are separate from the rest of the poem?

Exploring your own response

12 How successful is this poem in portraying a man's feelings after being rejected?

On the Departure Platform Thomas Hardy

Content and theme

1 This poem, like **Since there's no help . . .**, is about saying goodbye – but not necessarily because the relationship is over. Read the poem and think about:

- the situation that is being described
- what the poet is actually saying goodbye to.

Imagery

2 Thomas Hardy creates some haunting and vivid visual images to convey the scene and his feelings. Find images which suggest:

- the moment growing increasingly distant
- the scene at the railway station and their separation from it
- the girl moving away along the platform as he watches
- the girl as ghost-like.

Language

3 Find examples in the poem of the following:

- *repetition*
- *alliteration*
- *dialogue*.

For each example, explain why you think the poet has chosen the technique.

4 List or highlight all the adjectives the poet uses to describe the girl.

5 Do we get a clear idea of her as a person? If not, what ideas and images are associated with her? What might she represent?

Structure

6 The poem tells a story in *stanzas*. Summarise the content of each stanza.

7 Why has the poet finished each stanza with a short line? Does the length of the line reinforce its meaning? Why might Hardy have wanted to create a sense of something cut short?

Exploring your own response

8 Think about these statements and find evidence from the poem to back them up.

a The poem is about having to say goodbye to someone you love.
b The poem gives a strong sense of time and place.
c Young lovers feel apart from the rest of the world.
d The girl represents being young and in love.
e The girl represents innocence.
f The poem uses the lovers' farewell to reflect on the passing of youth.
g The poem is a sad one even though the lovers have not parted forever.

Compare

Compare this poem with **Since there's no help . . .**

- How does each convey the feelings of the poet about saying goodbye?
- How does each poem reveal more than is at first apparent?

Remember Christina Rossetti

and In the Mile End Road Amy Levy

Content and theme

1 These two poems are also about lovers parting.

a What sort of partings are described in each poem?
b How do the poets' perspectives differ?
c Who, if anyone, is addressed in each?

Imagery

2 What is suggested to you by the following images from each poem?

Remember	In the Mile End Road
• the silent land • hold me by the hand • half turn to go yet turning stay • darkness and corruption (corruption here refers to the decay of the body)	• Comes up the crowded street • that motion and that mien • that airy tread

Language and structure

Remember

3 When do you think this poem was intended to be read?

4 Find examples of language which might be meant to comfort, and which might upset a bereaved person. Do you think the poet really wants to be forgotten?

5 The poem repeats the word 'remember' five times, and then contrasts it with 'forget'. What is the effect of this?

6 Why do you think the poem is divided into two *stanzas*? Is there a change in focus?

7 Explore the use of *rhyme*. Can you find reinforcement and contrasts?

8 When instructions are given as orders this is called the *imperative*. Find examples.

In the Mile End Road

9 This poem takes the form of thoughts in the speaker's head. The poet uses language and *structure* to suggest the thoughts that might go through your head if you came across your lover by surprise. Find examples of:

> • sudden recognition   • use of exclamations   • use of questions.

10 Why does this approach help to keep the ending a surprise?

Exploring your own response

11 How do each of these two poems treat the idea of the death of a lover? Which do you find most moving, convincing, poetic and dramatic?

A Scherzo – A Shy Person's Wishes Dora Greenwell

Content and theme

1 In what ways is this poem about the poet cheering herself up? Could it also be considered a joke?

Imagery

2 The poem is largely made up of a list of images. These are grouped to suggest particular ideas. Find and brainstorm images that convey the following ideas:

- hidden and safe
- powerful and free
- remote
- deeply buried
- part of the natural world
- having a purpose.
- waiting to happen
- exotic

Language

3 The poet uses adjectives grouped in threes to describe the ideas suggested:

> - hidden, and safe, and bold
> - rooted, and firm, and deep
> - timid, and shy, and free
> - chainless, and tameless, and proud

What do these adjectives suggest about the way the poet sees herself?

4 The language suggests an interesting contrast between wanting to be hidden and wanting to be free. What is the poet saying about what it is like to be shy?

5 Find three examples of the poet using *assonance* and/or *alliteration*. Explore the effects of these techniques.

Structure

6 The poem is written as one long unbroken *stanza*, with a regular *rhythm* and *rhyme scheme*. Find and make a note of lines in the poem where:
- the regular *rhythm* and *rhyme* convey peace and order in nature
- the pace suggests freedom and energy
- the momentum builds up, suggesting a growing desperation to get away.

7 a Why do you think 'anywhere' is repeated twice in the last line?
  b What does the last line make you feel about the rest of the poem?
  c What does the last line suggest about the poet's situation?

Exploring your own response

8 What does this poem tell you about what it is like to be shy?

9 How does it suggest a rich and interesting inner life?

10 The poet fantasises in private about being natural, free, energetic, and having a purpose. What does this suggest about the way she has to be in her social life? Why might this be a particular issue for women living in the nineteenth century?

The Sick Rose William Blake

Content and theme

1 There are many possible interpretations of this poem. After a first reading, what does it seem to be about?

Imagery

2 Now concept-map the key *images* in the poem and see if you can arrive at your own interpretation. Look at the example in the Skills section on page 9. Then draw similar diagrams for:

- the invisible worm
- in the night
- thy bed of crimson joy
- the rose
- dark secret love.

3 Discuss your diagrams and ideas with others. Are there any common patterns or recurring associations?

Language

4 The language of **The Sick Rose** could be described as biblical and dramatic. Find examples of each from the poem.

5 It seems as if the poem is giving a coded warning or even a sermon. How does the language fit such a purpose?

6 How does the rhyme pattern work? What picture do the pairs of rhymed words create?

Structure

7 The poem is written in two *stanzas*. Is there a reason for this?

8 The *rhythm* and *rhyme scheme* are regular. How does this fit in with the possible purpose of the poem?

Exploring your own response

9 Consider the following possible interpretations and try to justify them, finding evidence from the poem. If your own interpretation does not fit in with these, create your own statements for others to justify.

a The poem warns women about sexually transmitted disease in an age when people were uneducated about sexual health and there were no cures available.

b The poem is about how repressed feelings can eat away at you – love should not be secret.

c The poem warns girls about the dangers of seduction and loss of innocence – but also shows how attractive it can seem.

Compare

Compare this poem with **A Scherzo**. How do both poets convey the idea of a secret inner life?

Sonnet 138 William Shakespeare
and **The Sun Rising** John Donne

Content and theme

1 Copy and complete the chart below to describe the interior world and the implied contrast with reality in each poem.

	Interior/lovers' world	Exterior/real world
Sonnet 138	He is young	
		She lies to him
		He pretends to believe her
The Sun Rising	Love is timeless	
		The sun is more powerful than he
	They are the most exotic and exciting thing in the world	
		There's a big world outside

Imagery

2 **The Sun Rising** starts with *images* of busy, reluctant people going about their daily lives. What do these images suggest? How are the lovers different?

3 Identify the images connected with exotic places, power and influence that follow. What do they suggest about the way being in love can make you feel?

Language

4 In **The Sun Rising** the poet seems to address the sun directly. Why does he call him a 'Busy old fool'?

5 Find some examples of *rhetorical questions* in **The Sun Rising**, e.g.'Why shouldst thou think?' What effect do these have? Who is the poet really addressing?

6 Both poems have a regular *rhyme scheme*. How do the pairs of rhyming words work together? Is there any difference between the rhyme schemes for each poem?

7 **Sonnet 138** contains a *pun* on the word 'lie' in the final lines. What two possible meanings could it have?

Compare

Compare these two
'worlds' with those
shown in **The Sick
Rose** and **A Scherzo**.

Structure

8 Both poems move towards a conclusion. Identify the stages.

Exploring your own response

9 Evaluate the ways in which each poet creates a sense of the lover's world.

Sonnet Elizabeth Barrett Browning

Content and theme

1 Read through the poem and identify:
- who is speaking
- who is being addressed
- what the situation/purpose is.

Imagery

2 In trying to express her feelings, the poet uses a range of *imagery*. Copy the chart and complete it with examples of images with the following associations.

Associations	Images
Religion/spirituality	'ideal Grace'
Day and night	
Childhood/simplicity	
Strength of feeling	

3 What is she trying to convey about the nature of her love through such images?

Language

4 The language in this poem is dramatic, often expressing extremes and contrasts in emotion. Look for words and phrases which demonstrate this.

5 How many times is 'I love thee' repeated? What effect does this have?

Structure

6 This poem is a *sonnet*. How far is this poem a typical sonnet in its:
- structure
- theme
- language?

7 The first part of the poem seems to suggest that the person the speaker is addressing is her God. How is this impression altered by the final lines?

Exploring your own response

8 How successful do you think this poem is in conveying the poet's feelings?

9 What view of romance and relationships is offered here? What is suggested about the importance of love?

The Unequal Fetters Anne Finch

Content and theme

1 This poem gives a woman's view of love and marriage. Sum up her attitude and give reasons for it. How does the title give a clue to what follows?

2 Who do you think is meant to read the poem? A lover? A wider audience? Men? Women? Both? Give reasons for your answers.

Imagery

3 Explore the following *images* and what they suggest in the poem:

> - time that's flying
> - youth for ever
> - lose those graces
> - spring of life
> - close prisoners
> - slaves of Hymen (getting married is like being sold into slavery).
> - begging love
> - length of all their chain

4 Which images seem to suggest similar ideas?

5 Which are common or *clichéd* images? Which are new and original?

Language and structure

6 Find examples of language which you feel to be poetic or dramatic. Why is such language appropriate for the purpose of the poem?

7 To achieve the regular *metre* and *rhyme scheme*, the poet has used some sentence *structures* which are more poetic than natural. How might you structure the following sentences in prose or when speaking? Rewrite them in modern-day speech.

> - Could we stop the time that's flying
> - To love would then be worth our cost
> - Marriage does but slightly tie men
> - Yield to be in fetters bound

8 How does the regular beat of the *metre* fit in with idea of women as slaves?

Exploring your own response

9 Find evidence from the poem to justify the following statements.

a The poet is angry about women's fate and men's treatment of women.
b The poet wants to show that this is not how it was meant to be.
c The poet uses a dramatic image of married women to show how powerful her feelings about this are.
d The poet wants to warn women off marriage.
e The poet wants to men to treat women better.

 Compare

- Compare the view of love in **The Unequal Fetters** to that in **How do I love thee?** How do the poets use dramatic images and language to achieve very different effects?

- Compare the view of relationships in **The Unequal Fetters** with that in **To His Coy Mistress**. What is suggested about the different ways in which men and women view love?

29

Faithless Sally Brown Thomas Hood

Genre and structure

1 Discuss the ways in which this poem is a typical *ballad*. Ballads

- are traditional folk songs or poems that tell a story
- focus on dramatic events
- don't give much background story or characters' motivation
- are traditionally heard or sung rather than read
- rhyme
- have refrains/choruses which comment on action or build mood
- are structured in *quatrains* with a 4,3,4,3 or 4,4,4,4 stress pattern
- build a story through dialogue and action
- don't identify the speakers of dialogue
- focus on one scene, then jump to another.

Language

2 This poem also uses *colloquial language*. Find some examples of this.

3 How does this language fit in with the theme/story/character and the genre?

They flee from me . . . Sir Thomas Wyatt

Content and theme

1 This poem offers another view of the behaviour of women in love. What impression is conveyed of the women and their behaviour?

Imagery and language

2 Thomas Wyatt creates an *extended image* of women as wild creatures who he has managed to tame. Find words and phrases that help to support this image.

3 The poet creates a vision of the past that is like a dream. How is this made clear?

4 The poet uses *antonyms* to create pictures of the past and present. Note down as many of these as you can.

Structure

5 The poem is written in three *stanzas*. Look at the content of each and explain why it is structured in this way.

6 What do the last two lines add to your understanding of the poem?

Exploring your response

7 What view of relationships, particularly of women's behaviour, is suggested in these two poems?

⇄ **Compare**

Find other poems in this section with similar and contrasting views. Explore the similarities and contrasts. Use the 'Comparing poems' guide in the Skills section on page 16 to help you.

Time and Change

The poems in this section explore the ways in which people, places and relationships can change over time.

Before reading the poems, work through these activities with a partner.

1 Take turns to describe your early memories, using these questions to guide you.
- How have you changed since you were a young child?
- How has your view of the world and understanding of it changed? Did you believe in anything then that you now don't?
- How do you think you will continue to change as a person as you get older?

2 Look at these statements and discuss how far you believe them.
- a Childhood is the best time of life.
- b Human nature never changes.
- c True love never dies.
- d Changes in relationships and friendships are hard to cope with.
- e Nothing lasts for ever.

Reading the poems for the first time

Work with a partner or in a group for this activity.

> Choose two or three poems to read through on your own.

↓

> Do any of the statements above seem to apply to the poems? Make a note of which statement seems to fit which poem, and why you think so.

↓

> Now get together with another person or group. Tell them your thoughts about the links between the statements and the poems, and ask for theirs. If you have read the same poems, compare your ideas. If you have read different poems, make a note of each other's ideas.

↓

> Now move on to compare, or share with the class. Can you group all the poems under different statements, or are there any which don't seem to fit? If there are, try to make up your own statements for these.

I Remember, I Remember Thomas Hood

Content and theme

1 Read through the poem. What sort of memories is the poem conjuring up? What are your first impressions of the childhood he describes? What do you think he misses more – the place, or the child he used to be?

Imagery

2 Match the *images* below to the technique descriptions with arrows – the first one has been done for you. Then reflect on what impressions these images give you.

Image	Technique
the sun/Came peeping in at morn	Use of senses
roses, red and white	Personification
The violets, and the lily-cups	Metaphor
the air must rush as fresh/To swallows on the wing	Visual detail/ colour
My spirit flew in feathers	

Language

3 Find words or phrases which create an impression of:
- a friendly childhood world
- restlessness/stress
- freedom
- despair
- a child's perspective.

4 How does the use of *exclamation* in the final line of each stanza suggest the poet is distressed?

5 What does the final line suggest about one difference between children and adults? Why does the poet find this so upsetting?

Structure

6 The poem is structured into four *stanzas*. What is each stanza about? Create your own flowchart to track the poet's thoughts through to the poem's climax.

7 The poem has a very regular *rhythm* and *rhyme scheme*. Do you agree with the following statements? If so, find evidence from the poem to support each one.

a The regularity is hypnotic, taking the poet back to his childhood days.

b The regular rhythm matches the simple language – it creates a nursery rhyme impression.

c The phrase 'I remember, I remember' is repeated like a spell to conjure the past.

Exploring your own response

8 How successful is the poet in creating a vision of childhood?

9 What attitude to the past is evident in this poem?

Into my heart . . . A. E. Housman

Content and theme

1. Read through the poem. What sort of place is described? Highlight or make a note of any words or phrases that seem interesting or striking.

Imagery

2. The *images* in this poem build a picture of an idealised landscape. Brainstorm individual images to examine how the poet does this. Here is an example:

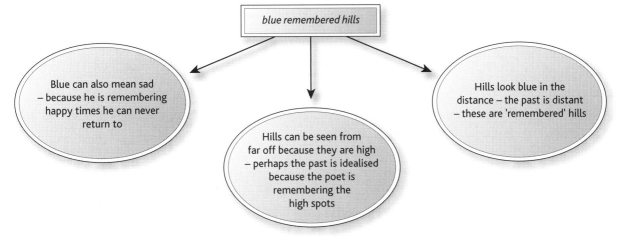

Explore these images in the same way:

- Into my heart an air that kills
- yon far country
- What spires, what farms are those?
- The happy highways
- the land of lost content

⇄ Compare

- How do **Into my heart . . .** and **I Remember, I Remember** create an ideal past?
- What are the similarities and differences in the poets' attitudes to the past, and how are these suggested?

Language

3. The poem describes an idealised, fairy-tale landscape. The language reflects this in that it is poetic rather than conversational. Find examples of this type of language.

Structure

4. This poem is divided into two *stanzas* – the first sets up a mystery and asks questions, the second provides the answer. This could reflect a folk-tale tradition where a traveller in a strange land asks questions about where he is or asks for directions, and receives an answer which is a riddle.

Summarise the question and answer. Why is the answer of no use to a 'traveller'?

Exploring your own response

5. How does Housman's poem create a sense of the past? What does it suggest about the way people see the past in relation to the present?

Spring and Fall Gerard Manley Hopkins
and The Gray Folk Edith Nesbit

Content and theme

1 Both these poems convey the changes people go through as they grow older. What sort of changes are described in each? Are they for the better or worse?

Imagery

2 Both poems use some natural and some supernatural *imagery*.

  a Discuss the images listed in the table below and any others you find interesting.

  b What mood do the patterns of imagery in each poem help create?

Spring and Fall	The Gray Folk
• Goldengrove unleaving	• lonely in the last year's corn
• worlds of wanwood leafmeal	• the green fields of yesterday
• ghost guessed	• like the faces of the dead

Language

3 Find examples of the language features listed below from each poem and comment on their effect. Add any others you find interesting.

  - *alliteration*
  - **internal** *rhyme*
  - *assonance*
  - *repetition*
  - listing
  - *rhyme which reinforces meaning.*

Structure

4 Which of the following statements can be applied to each poem?

  a This poem uses *enjambment* to create a strong sense of flow.
  b This poem uses *stanzas* to describe progress from the outside to the inside.
  c This poem is formed of questions and answers.
  d This poem has a slow, solemn *rhythm* which fits the mood.

Exploring your own response

5 In both poems there is a sense of loss. Explain, using evidence from the poems, what you think the loss is and how this feeling is created.

 Compare

- What similarities and differences can you find in the attitudes to time and change in **I Remember, I Remember** and **Into my heart ...?**
- How these are conveyed by the respective poets?

The Listeners Walter de la Mare

Content and theme

1 **The Listeners** is narrated like an old folk-tale or ghost story. Who do you think the Traveller is and why is he calling?

Imagery

2 The poet builds atmosphere by creating strong *images* of sights and sounds. What do the examples below suggest to you? How do they work? Can you find other examples to explore?

- Knocking on the moonlit door
- a host of phantom listeners
- that voice from the world of men
- Stood thronging the faint moonbeams on the dark stair
- air stirred and shaken
- echoing through the shadowiness of the still house
- the sound of iron on stone
- the silence surged softly backward

---

3 Find clues in the poem that suggest the appearance and situation of the house.

Language

4 Read the poem closely and make a note of words and phrases you might expect to find in a fairy tale and in a ghost story. How do these help to build atmosphere and create expectations?

5 Look at the poet's use of *dialogue*. How does it:
a make the scene more dramatic and
b give us clues about the story?

Structure

6 This poem has a regular *rhythm* and *rhyme scheme*. Work out the pattern of stresses per line and the pattern of rhyme. Why do these make this poem excellent for reading aloud? How do they help to entertain the listener?

Exploring your own response

7 How successful is the poet in creating a sense of atmosphere and mystery in **The Listeners**? What does it leave you wondering?

Compare

- How do both this poem and **Ozymandias** create a picture and lead the reader to wonder about the past?
- How do both this poem and **The Gray Folk** create a sense of guilt or obligation through the supernatural?
- How do both this poem and **The Gray Folk** use rural imagery?

Ozymandias Percy Bysshe Shelley

Content and theme

1 Like **The Listeners**, this poem creates a strong visual image and leaves the reader wondering about the past. It also reflects on human pride and power. What do you think the main message of the poem is?

Imagery

2 What pictures are conjured in your mind by the following quotations?

> - a traveller from an antique land
> - Two vast and trunkless legs of stone
> - a shattered visage
> - sneer of cold command
> - stamped on these lifeless things
> - Look on my works, ye Mighty, and despair!
> - that colossal wreck
> - boundless and bare/The lone and level sands stretch far away

3 What do the descriptions given in the poem tell you about:

- the sort of ruler that Ozymandias was
- what used to be on the site surrounding the statue
- what may have happened to it?

4 Who does seem to have made a lasting mark? Why might the poet highlight the role of the sculptor? Does it suggest anything about his hopes for his own work?

Language

5 Find words and phrases in the poem which suggest:

- desertion   • power   • pride.

6 Look at the poet's use of adjectives and *alliteration*. What do these add?

Structure

7 The poem uses *dialogue* and *exclamation* to tell its story. How does this make it more immediate and dramatic?

8 Look at the *juxtaposition* of Ozymandias's statement, and the next line, 'Nothing beside remains'. What effect does this have?

9 Look at the use of punctuation and *enjambment*. How does this help create flow and pauses? What is the effect?

Exploring your own response

10 How successfully does Shelley create:

- a sense of place   • a sense of mystery   • a moral point?

11 Do you agree with his view that artists might be more important than kings in history?

Compare

- Compare the poets' treatment of setting and creation of mystery in **Ozymandias, The Listeners** and **The Gray Folk**.
- Compare the poets' treatment of the relationship between the past and the present in **Ozymandias** and **Into my heart . . .** and **I Remember, I Remember**.

To the Virgins . . . Robert Herrick

and **The Darkling Thrush** Thomas Hardy

Content and theme

1 Both these poems are concerned with the passage of time. What are the poet's particular concerns in each? What is worrying them? Is there any hope in either poem? Is the poet addressing a particular audience?

Imagery

2 Explore the *images* below, and add any more you find interesting. Which images are connected with nature? Which images are associated with people/humanity?

To the Virgins, to Make Much of Time	The Darkling Thrush
• Gather ye rosebuds while ye may • this same flower that smiles to-day/ To-morrow will be dying • glorious lamp of heaven • nearer he's to setting • youth and blood are warmer	• Frost was spectre-gray • mankind that haunted nigh • The Century's corpse • His crypt the cloudy canopy • The wind his death-lament • frail, gaunt, and small

Compare

- Compare the treatment of atmosphere and time in these two poems with **The Gray Folk** and **The Listeners**.
- Compare the treatment of the themes of time passing, youth and age, with **Into my heart . . .** and **I Remember, I Remember**.
- How do the poets deal with time and the inevitability of death and decay compared with **Ozymandias** and **Spring and Fall**?

Language

3 **To the Virgins** is written in the form of instruction or advice. Identify the language features that tell you this.

4 **The Darkling Thrush** is more personal and thoughtful. What suggests these are the poet's personal thoughts?

5 Both poems use poetic rather than conversational language. Find three examples from each to demonstrate this. Why do you think the poets chose such language?

6 Look at the use of *rhyme* in each poem. Find paired rhymes which **a** reinforce and **b** contrast the meaning in each poem. How do these help to convey the meaning?

7 Hardy uses sound as well as visual description to paint his picture of the desolate countryside. Identify some of his techniques for doing this and explain the effects.

Structure

8 These poems have different *rhythms* and pace. Describe how rhythm and pace are used in each poem, explaining how each is suitable for the mood or message.

9 Explain why each poem is structured into its pattern of stanzas. Trace the progression and change of focus through the stanzas in each poem.

Exploring your response

10 Compare the key message in each poem and the different ways in which the poets have conveyed it.

The Latest Decalogue Arthur Hugh Clough

Content and theme

1 This poem offers a cynical view of why we should keep the Ten Commandments. Why do you think it is called **The Latest Decalogue**? On your first reading, how would you describe the poet's view of human behaviour? Do you think the poet's view would still apply today?

Language

2 Rather than write out the Ten Commandments as they appear in the Bible, the poet has altered the wording slightly to make them fit his *rhythm* and *rhyme scheme*.
  a Find examples from the poem that sound like original biblical language.
  b Why is it important that he does this **a** for recognition by the reader and **b** for the *tone* of the poem?

3 How does he make the reasons given for keeping the Commandments sound like truths too?
  a Do they share any language or *structures* with the Commandments themselves?
  b Does he contrast this with any less formal language?
  Find examples and discuss the effects and why the poet might have done this.

4 Link the quotations given below with the correct meaning, as shown in the example.

Quotation	Meaning
• except the currency • keep the world thy friend • all/From whom advancement may befall • strive/Officiously to keep alive • Advantage rarely comes of it • tradition/Approves all forms of competition	• Reputation and image matter. • Doing good to another is interfering. • It is human nature to try and get what others have. • Money is the only thing of real value and should be the focus of your life. • Only bother with the people who can do something for you. • Don't do anything that you won't get something out of.

Structure

5 This poem is written as one *stanza*, but within it there is a clearly balanced structure. What is each Commandment followed by?

6 What effect does inserting a pause (a semi-colon) after each Commandment have?

7 The poem has a regular and bouncy rhythm. How does this fit in with the tone?

Exploring your own response

8 Look up these words in a dictionary or thesaurus if you are not familiar with them, and then discuss the ways in which they could be used to describe the poem:
  • satirical • cynical • misanthropic.

On the Times Anon.

Content and theme

1 What does the title suggest the poem will be about? What view of society does the poet offer?

Language

2 Make a list of all the words that sound the same as modern words and but are spelled differently. Write down their meaning **a** in the modern sense and **b** in the poem, if this is different. Here are some to get you started:

> • consciens   • litel   • theves   • bost

3 Now list all the words that seem strange because they are no longer in common use. Can you work out their meaning from the context?

Imagery

4 The poem offers a series of visual *images* connected with putting on a show. What can we work out about the fashions and social position from the images below?

> • a gallant penylese
> • Grete countenance and smalle wages
> • Many gentilemen and few pages
> • Wide gownes and large sleves
> • Wel besene and strong theves
> • Much bost of their clothes

Structure

5 The *structure* of this poem and **The Latest Decalogue** have features in common. Both are structured with statements of contrast which maintain a constant balance throughout the poem. In **On the Times**, what opposites can you find?

6 Why do you think the poet repeats the word 'many'? What is the effect of this?

7 The poem gives a busy, crowded list of examples of people who put show before substance. Why do you think the poet chooses to give this impression?

Exploring your own response

8 Which of the words given in question 8 on **The Latest Decalogue** also applies to this poem?

9 Who do you think is the target of this poet?

This poem was written in the fifteenth century. Since then, the English language has changed and developed, and spelling has become standardised, so the words and some of the spellings will be unfamiliar to you.

⇄ **Compare**

Compare the view of society offered by this poem and by **The Latest Decalogue**.

• Which aspects of either poem could still apply to society today?

• Are they comments on human nature in general, or are they specific to their times?

A Song Laetitia Pilkington

and Death the Leveller James Shirley

Content and theme

1 What human experience is described in each of these poems? What comment does each poet make about rich and successful people?

Language and imagery

G 2 **Death the Leveller** creates some powerful visual *images*. Find three that you think are particularly interesting and concept-map their effects. (Look back at page 9 to remind yourself how to do this.)

3 **Death the Leveller** uses some words that have more than one meaning or association. What meanings can you identify for these words or phrases?

> - scythe and spade
> - reap
> - garlands

4 **A Song** uses less visual imagery but it achieves some similar effects. Concept-map the images created by the words and phrases below:

> - an occupation
> - ensnare
> - science
> - Bid to Truth a bold defiance

Compare

- Compare the poets' views on humanity and society, moral comment, tone and purpose with those in **The Latest Decalogue, On the Times** and **Ozymandias**.
- Compare the use of mood, tone and imagery in **Death the Leveller** with **The Darkling Thrush, The Gray Folk** and **The Listeners**.

Structure

G 5 Both poems are structured into three *stanzas*.

   a For each poem, identify the shifts in focus for each new stanza.

   b How does each poem use the three-stanza pattern to introduce, develop and conclude the line of thought?

G 6 Both poems use a regular *rhyme scheme*. Make a note of the pairs of rhyming words. How does each poet use rhyme to **a** reinforce and **b** contrast?

G 7 **Death the Leveller** breaks the regular *metre* with two shorter lines in each stanza. What ideas are expressed in the shorter lines? How are the ideas connected to the length of the lines?

Exploring your own response

8 How does each poet convey their view of humanity? Which features of each poem do you find most interesting?

Woak Hill William Barnes

Content and theme

1 This poem tells a story. Read it through and decide what the story is about and what view of love, death and relationships is being offered.

Language

2 The poem is written in a West Country dialect. Read the poem aloud in pairs. Does it help you to understand it?

3 Why do you think the poet has chosen to use *dialect* and *colloquialisms*?

4 Make a note of or highlight any words that seem unfamiliar. Try to work out the possible meaning from the context or from the sounds of the words.

Imagery

5 **Woak Hill** creates *images* to suggest the following ideas:
- the countryside/rural setting
- their marriage
- the man's home
- the woman's spirit.

Find examples for each to brainstorm and explore. Describe the way each of your examples works.

Structure

6 **Woak Hill** tells a story in *stanzas*. Read through the poem and decide which stanzas:
- set the scene
- describe character
- move the story on
- reflect on events.

7 When you read through the poem, think about the *rhythm*. Which of these adjectives could be used to describe it:
- steady
- slow
- frantic
- regular
- broken
- up-beat
- hypnotic
- depressing?

8 Look at the final line in each stanza. How is *rhyme* created here? How does this help bind the poem together?

Exploring your own response

9 In what ways do all these elements fit together:
- the rural setting
- the type of story
- the main character
- the use of dialect?

10 How does the poet create a sense of:
- time and change
- the nature of relationships
- other worlds/realities?

Compare

Compare **Woak Hill** with **Death the Leveller** for the poets' attitudes to death; with **I Remember, I Remember** for the relationship of the past to the present; with **The Listeners** for supernatural elements and setting; and with **A Poison Tree** and **The Poison Flower** for images of relationships.

Dreams Robert Herrick

1 Before you read the poem, make some notes describing:
- a dream or nightmare you can remember having recently
- your day at school so far.

Then share your experiences of each with a partner. How similar were your daytime experiences? How different were your dreams?

Content and theme

2 Read through the poem.
- **a** In what ways is this poem about different kinds of reality?
- **b** What two worlds are suggested and what is the difference between them?

Language and imagery

3 Because this poem is so short, the language has to work hard to convey the meaning. Look at these words and phrases, and consider their effects:

- we are all . . . each one
- hurled/By dreams
- by day . . . by night
- a several world

⇄ Compare

Compare **Dreams** with **The Gray Folk, Into my heart . . ., The Listeners, I Remember, I Remember** and **Woak Hill** for the ways in which they suggest altered states and different worlds.

Structure

4 How does the two line *structure* reflect the subject matter?

5 What examples of contrasting pairs can you find in the poem?

6 How does the poet use *punctuation/enjambment* to create pauses and continuity?

Exploring your own response

7 Look back at the Content and theme question. How does the poet suggest:
- common experiences
- separate experiences
- lack of control and violence?

8 Which world seems most comfortable? Which is the most exciting or threatening? Give reasons for your answers.

A Poison Tree William Blake

and The Poison Flower Mary Coleridge

Content and theme

1 These poems could be described as *allegories*. What is the story in each? What suggests these stories are *metaphors* rather than real events?

2 What do you think each poet wanted us to learn from their poem?

Imagery

3 Find garden images from each poem to support the following statements.
  a Relationships need careful tending, like plants.
  b We need love to thrive like plants need the sun.
  c Bad thoughts and actions act like weedkiller on plants.
  d Bad people in society are like weeds in the garden.

4 Although both poems seem to use the same kind of imagery, there are different ideas behind them. For example, the apple in Blake's poem suggests the story of the garden of Eden and the story of Snow White. How do these stories add to our understanding of the poem?

Language

5 Find pairs of *rhymes* that reinforce and contrast meaning in each poem.

6 **A Poison Tree** uses some language and *structures* that sound biblical. What does this add to the poem? How does this fit in with the poet's purpose?

7 Explore the effect of these phrases:

A Poison Tree	The Poison Flower
• I sunned it with smiles	• their fiery foe
• he knew that it was mine	• dull disgrace
• glad I see	• languished and grew old

8 **A Poison Tree** has a simple and regular *rhyme* and *rhythm*, almost like a nursery rhyme. Why might Blake have wanted to create this impression?

Structure

9 Both poems tell a story in four *stanzas*. How is the story developed in each stanza?

Exploring your own response

10 How do both poems use garden images to explore human relationships?

Extension

Both poems use an *extended image* of a garden. Make a list of all the garden references in each. Now explore stories and traditions associated with roses and lilies.

Generations

OPENING LINES

The poems in this section are as varied as families can be – but they are all about relationships between generations, for example, the love between a parent and a child.

1 Before reading the poems, discuss these statements with a partner. Do you agree or disagree with each statement? Give reasons for your views.

  a Children should take care of their parents when they get old.
  b Girls love babies.
  c Life was simpler in our parents' and grandparents' time.
  d Parents are over-protective.
  e Dads are heroes to small boys.

2 Work in a group of four. Take three or four poems each, and then copy and complete a chart like the one below with your analysis of each poem.

Poem and poet	Generations involved	What the poem is about	Voice (who is speaking)	Audience (who is being spoken to)	Mood/tone (angry, loving, sad etc)

3 Now share your notes with the rest of your group and complete the chart for all the poems. You can add or change details at this stage. If you have time, reading the poems aloud will help you.

4 Next, compare your chart with other groups in the class.

5 Finally, choose two poems from the section to compare. What similarities can you find? What differences? Refer to the 'Comparing Poems' activity in the Skills section (page 16) to help you do this.

Poem Simon Armitage

Content and theme

Look back at the chart on page 8 of the Skills section.

1 What suggests that this is a poem about an ordinary sort of man?

2 Which tells us more about the poem – the title or the last line?

Imagery

3 The poem uses simple visual *imagery* to build a picture of this man in relation to his family. Find images of:
- the man's strength
- the man's traditional role in the family
- the man's care for his family
- the man's temper.

Language

4 **Poem** makes use of *colloquial language*. Below are some examples. What is suggested by each?

> - tossed it
> - tucked . . . up
> - his mum
> - blubbed

5 Look at the adverbs of frequency (words that tell us how often something happens) in the poem, e.g. 'always'. Which adverbs are used to describe good actions and which are used to describe bad actions?

Structure

6 The poem starts with the word 'And'. This is repeated at the start of many other lines. Why might the poet have wanted to:
- use such repetition
- create a sense of ritual or of something that is always done in the same way?

7 This poem is a *sonnet*. Identify the features of the poem that are typical of and those that differ from a traditional sonnet.

Exploring your own response

8 How successfully do you think Simon Armitage has suggested:
- the man's ordinariness
- that people are rarely all good or all bad
- that family life is made up of small rituals?

Extension

The phrase 'when they looked back' suggests that the man has died and his life is being discussed. Imagine your class is divided into demons and angels. Decide which you will be and then argue your case for his soul, using evidence from the poem.

The Flowers Selima Hill

Content and theme

1 Read through the poem and decide:
- who is speaking
- what is being described
- what the mood/feelings in the poem are.

Imagery

2 This poem uses some vivid visual *imagery*, as well as *simile* and *metaphor*. Copy and complete a chart like the one below to help you explore some images in the poem. Add any more you can find.

Image	Type	This image suggests
like a little dog, I followed her	simile	
scraped the moss from the stone		That the grave had been neglected
making his bed in the morning		
moving apart/and coming together again,/ in and out of the ruts		

Language

3 Find words and phrases in the poem that suggest:
- nature
- care
- neglect
- simplicity.

How do these contribute to the poem's mood?

Compare

Compare the different pictures of family relationships created in this poem and **Poem** by Simon Armitage. How do the different techniques work to create contrasts?

Form

4 The poem is written in three *stanzas*, which work like three parts of a short story – before, during and after. What events does each stanza describe? What feelings are created in each stanza?

5 This poem is gentle and flowing. To help achieve this, the poet frequently uses *enjambment*. Find some examples of this and explain why you think it works well.

6 Now look at the way the poet has used punctuation to introduce pauses. Again, find examples of this and explain why you think a pause is effective in each case.

Exploring your own response

7 How effectively do the images, language and form of this poem work together?

Follower Seamus Heaney and **Imitations** Dannie Abse

The next two poems you are going to explore and compare also deal with family relationships – in this case, fathers and sons. The table below suggests features you should look for in each poem.

1 When you have identified these features, use a concept map (see Skills section, page 9) or discussion to explore their effects.

Features	Follower	Imitations
Subject/ theme	Who is speaking? Mood Attitude	Who is speaking? Mood Attitude
Images	• The rural scene • His father's size • His feelings about his father • Visual and aural *images*	• Nature – beginnings and temporariness • *Metaphors* for adolescence • Visual and tactile *images*
Language	Words which suggest: • effort • skill • his father's size • irritation. Use of *assonance* Use of *rhyme* Past and present tense	Words which suggest: • distance between them • repeated patterns • a poetic view. Use of *assonance* Use of *alliteration* Use of *rhyme* Past and present tense
Form	How the story is divided into *stanzas* The role of the final stanza The *rhythm* – how created through *metre*, punctuation and *enjambment*	How the story is divided into *stanzas* The role of the final stanza The *rhythm* – how created through *metre*, punctuation and *enjambment*

2 When you have found and thought about a range of features in each poem you can begin to consider them together. The following questions may help you.

a In what ways are both poems about generations?
b In what ways are both poems about growing old?
c Whose feelings are explored in each poem?
d How does the vision of nature in each poem add to the mood?
e How does each poet *structure* his stanzas?
f What are the similarities in the ways that the poets use language and structure?

You're Sylvia Plath

Content and theme

1 The speaker's voice and the audience are key to understanding this poem. In it, a mother-to-be addresses her unborn child. On your first reading, how do you think she feels about the pregnancy and her baby?

Imagery

2 The poem contains a collection of *similes* and *metaphors* the poet has used to convey her thoughts and feelings about her baby. Some suggest similar feelings. Copy and complete a chart like the one below, adding any other similar *images*.

Images suggesting	Example	Associations
Fun/excitement	Clownlike	Circus, fun, tumbling around
	Fourth/Of July	
Evolution	Gilled like a fish	Early life had gills – evolution
Underwater life	creel of eels	Unborn babies float in amniotic fluid
Contentment		
New start	Australia	
Mystery/anticipation		
Life renewing		

Language and structure

3 Because the poem is made up of a series of images, Plath uses sound as well as linked images to help bind it together. Two noticeable techniques are internal *rhyme* and *assonance*. Find patterns of repeated sounds, and underline them, as below:

> • Thumbs-down on the dodo's mode = repeated 'd' and 'o' sounds
> • A creel of eels, all ripples = repeated 'e' and 'l' sounds

Form

4 The poem has an upbeat bouncy *rhythm*, reflecting the mother's feelings about her baby. To explore how the rhythm is achieved, look for examples of:
- length of phrases within lines and use of punctuation
- use of long and short vowels to vary pace.

Exploring your own response

5 How well do you think this poem conveys the poet's feelings of:
- joy   • anticipation   • mystery   • wonder?

Baby-sitting Gillian Clarke

Content and theme

1 Not all feelings about babies are to do with joy and love. Read the poem and decide:
- what the situation is
- what the poet's feelings are
- what she imagines the baby's feelings are.

Imagery

2 This poem uses some strong visual and aural *images*. What pictures and feelings are suggested by each example below? Discuss them with a partner or create a concept map – see Skills section, page 9.

- hot, midnight rage
- stream disgustingly
- the lover cold in lonely/Sheets
- the bleached bone in the terminal ward
- the monstrous land
- milk-familiar comforting
- snuffly . . . bubbling sleep

Language

3 Gillian Clarke uses rich and dramatic language to describe what she imagines the baby's feelings to be. When she describes her own feelings, however, her language is quite different. Match each quotation below to the correct feeling and then explain your decisions. Finally, add any other examples you can find.

Quotation	Feeling
a strange room	Only mothers really love their babies
the wrong baby	Disgust
I don't love/This baby	Fear
a perfectly acceptable child	Detachment
She will hate me	Unfamiliarity
It will not come. It will not come.	

Structure

4 The poem is divided into two *stanzas*. Describe the focus of each stanza.

5 The poet uses *enjambment* and pauses. How do these aspects work together to create an impression of thoughts running through the baby-sitter's head? You could comment on the use of present tense here too.

6 Why do you think the poet has used repetition in the last line?

Exploring your own response

7 What techniques has the poet used to describe the baby-sitter's and the baby's feelings? How successful do you think she has been?

8 Do you think this is an accurate picture of a baby-sitter's feelings for a child?

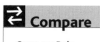
Compare

Compare **Baby-sitting** with **You're**.

These two poems offer further reflections on babies, and parents' feelings about their children.

To Edwin, at Eight Months Steve Ellis

and Clocks Gillian Clarke

Content and theme

1 Both poems focus on a child learning about the world around them. For each, think about how the parent describes their baby's learning and the parents' feelings about it.

Imagery

2 Explore or brainstorm the *images* below. What do they suggest to the reader? Can you see any links or patterns in the images?

To Edwin, at Eight Months	Clocks
• getting limbs/to agree to government • insurrectionary beetle • in a semaphore frenzy • wait . . . for your self to arrive • A fork in your future • scarper like scoutcubs / to feed your flame	• I teach him to tell the time / by dandelion • He blows me a field of gold / from the palm of his hand • The sun goes down in the sea • and the moon's translucent • and sand's/soft treachery underfoot • the full-blown moon

Language

3 Which of the poems uses the features below? Look for an example of each and then think about its effect.

- *alliteration*
- *dramatic language*
- *rhyme*
- *onomatopoeia*
- *dialogue*
- romantic language
- domestic language
- *assonance*

Structure

4 The *structure* of **To Edwin** . . . shows the stages in the poet's thoughts during the course of three *stanzas* – what he first thought, what he came to realise, and how the realisation affected him. Summarise his thoughts for each stanza.

5 **Clocks** captures moments in the day and the stanzas show afternoon moving to evening. How does Clarke suggest time?

Exploring your own response

6 What contrasting impressions of parents' feelings are created in these two poems? How have these impressions been achieved?

I Remember, I Remember Philip Larkin

Content and theme

1 In this poem, a chance occurrence leads the poet to think of his childhood. What happens to jog his memory and what sort of feelings are evoked?

Imagery

2 Many of the images in this poem are drawn from the sort of ideal childhood depicted in films and traditional children's books. Make a list of all the books and films you know which show an ideal childhood, e.g. *The Darling Buds of May*, *Swallows and Amazons*, *Cider With Rosie*, *The Famous Five*.

3 Now look at the descriptions below and find quotations from the poem which match each one.

a A child genius

b A warm and supportive family

c A good-looking family

d Family jokes

e A romantic first sexual experience

f Talent recognised at an early age

Language

4 Make a list of the negative *images* set against the idealised view of childhood. What is the overall effect?

5 What do the phrases below suggest about the way Larkin sees his home town and his childhood? Look at the underlined words in particular.

> • I wasn't even clear
>
> • I sat back, <u>staring</u> at my boots
>
> • my childhood was <u>unspent</u>
>
> • I wanted to <u>retort</u>

6 *Dialogue* is a feature of this poem. Why do you think the poet has chosen to use dialogue? What do the spoken words add to the poem?

Structure

7 This poem is organised into *stanzas*, but lines run over between stanzas in the same way that sentences run over between lines. What might the poet be suggesting about the nature of thought and memory?

8 Why do you think the last line is set apart from the others?

Exploring your own response

9 The poem creates a depressing and resentful view of childhood, by focusing on all the things the poet has read about in books, that ought to have been his and weren't. How successfully do you think he has contrasted his own childhood with the ideal?

The Tune the Old Cow Died Of Norman Nicholson

Content and theme

1 In this poem, like **I Remember, I Remember**, a 'trigger' is used to reflect on the past and present. What is the 'trigger' here'? What sorts of memories are evoked?

Imagery

2 Like **I Remember, I Remember**, this poem contains idealised *images* and a contrast with reality. Here, the poet looks at both sides of country life as well as contrasting country with town. Find *images* which match the statements given below.

   a Town life is claustrophobic.
   b Town life is dirty and unhealthy.
   c The countryside is lush.
   d The pace of life is relaxed.
   e The sights and sounds of nature add beauty to life.
   f Country life is harsh.
   g Poverty is the same wherever you live.
   h Poverty is stressful.

Language

3 Look at the examples below of the poet using sounds to help convey a vivid impression. Describe the effects each example has.

> - Shut in by slate
> - back street/Blocked...Barred
> - crags of slag
> - The toot of the flute
> - The humdrum hum of the bees
> - squeaked...scream...steam

Structure

4 This poem is written in two long *stanzas*. The first contrasts city life with a country ideal. Why has the poet created a second stanza for the next part?

5 Read the poem aloud to yourself. What do you notice about the *rhyme scheme*? Find pairs of rhyming words and see if they reinforce each other's meaning or contrast it.

6 The pace of this poem is brisk but slightly jerky with some short lines and some longer ones. What does this suggest – joy? anger? confusion? Are there any changes in pace? Where and why?

Exploring your own response

7 What do you think is the strongest feeling to emerge from this poem?

⇄ Compare

Compare this poem with **I Remember, I Remember**. How does each deal with idealisation of the past?

Long Distance Tony Harrison
and A Short Film Ted Hughes

Both poems describe responses to the death of family members, and the ways in which memories can affect you.

Content and theme

1 Describe briefly the situation each poet is writing about. Do there seem to be any differences in mood, *tone* or feeling in the poems?

Imagery

2 Both poems use patterns of *imagery* to convey a central feeling or idea. **Long Distance** uses domestic images and **A Short Film** contains images of a bomb. For each poem:

a Find all the examples that you can that fit into the pattern of imagery.
b Consider the effect of each image separately. Then describe the effect of the images combined. How does the pattern help to convey the poem's feeling and/or message?

Language

3 Using the Glossary to help you identify language features, consider the use of language in the examples below for each poem. The following questions may help.

a What does each example suggest?
b What does it add to the poem as a whole?

Long Distance	A Short Film
• Dad	• happy remembering
• still raw love	• too young
• blight of disbelief	• body-bomb
• He *knew*	• long-term
• just popped out	• *repetition* of 'a few' and 'skipping'
• my new black leather phone book	• made out of mist and smudge
• your name	• your grave inside us
• disconnected number	• a flash of fine sweat

Structure

4 Each of the poems comprises four *stanzas*. Look at what is described in each stanza and try to explain why each poem is organised in this way.

5 Look at the use of punctuation and find examples where each poet has:

- created an effective pause
- created a flow of lines that you think works well.

Give reasons for your choice of examples.

Exploring your own response

5 How do these poems convey different aspects of bereavement? Which do you think is more moving? More powerful?

Anseo Paul Muldoon

Content and theme

1 This poem is about how experiences in childhood can affect what we become in adulthood. Read through the poem and make a note of what Joseph experienced as a child, and what he is doing as an adult.

Imagery

2 **Anseo** captures moments from the past vividly. Think about or create a concept map for the examples below (see Skills section page 9). What does each suggest?

- And raise your hand
  As your name occurred
- knowing looks/A nod
  and a wink
- whittled down to a whip-lash
- Its twist of red and yellow lacquers
  Sanded and polished
- he had engraved his initials on it
- In a secret camp
  On the other side of the mountain

Language

3 The poet has written **Anseo** in a conversational style, but many of the words and phrases carry a deeper meaning. What is suggested by the following:

- And where's our little Ward-of-court?
- To weigh up for himself
- After a while, nothing was spoken
- as a matter of course
- Making things happen
- His volunteers

4 The title of the poem means 'here and now'. Why do you think the poet might have chosen this title?

Structure

5 The poem is structured in three *stanzas*. Look at the content of each stanza. How does the focus change in each?

6 The line length and use of punctuation help to create a flowing conversational *tone*. Find examples of line endings and punctuation being used to create pauses, and explain why you think Paul Muldoon has done this.

Exploring your own response

7 This poem reflects on the ways in which childhood experience can shape adult life. Look at these statements and justify them, using evidence from the poem. How strongly are the ideas conveyed?

a The old school system was cruel.
b Children will accept cruelty when they can't fight it.
c Even when you are beaten down you can still take pride in yourself.
d Oppressed people will fight back eventually.
e Suffering can make people stronger.
f What we experience as children shapes what we become as adults.

 Extension

The poet could be linking the cruel and oppressive Master to English rule of Ireland. If that is so, what might Joe Ward represent? What do you think the poem's message is?

To Carry the Child Stevie Smith

Content and theme

1. You may have heard the phrase 'inner child'. What does this poem suggest about paying attention to or having an 'inner child'?

Imagery

2. Stevie Smith uses a series of contrasting *images* to suggest the differences between being a child and being an adult. Find the contrasts in the poem, and add more, to complete a chart like the one below. Then explain how the contrasts work. What sort of picture do the images present of adults and children?

Child	Adult	Explanation
defenceless	despises, frozen	
easy in feeling		
	sees no colours	
the eye of an anarchist	carapace	

Language

3. The language in this poem is formal and *stylised*. It does not sound like everyday spoken language, but is more like a speech or a sermon. Find examples that help to create this impression, by use of:

- repetition
- biblical phrasing
- formal phrasing
- direct address to audience
- impersonal subject/object
- use of *vocative* ('Oh . . .').

Structure

4. The poem is structured into a series of short *stanzas* which contain pronouncements or statements. How does this structure support the ideas and impressions created by the language?

5. Can you think of any other texts that use similar language and structure?

Exploring your own response

6. Compare this poem with **Anseo** by Paul Muldoon.

   a What are the similarities and differences in what they have to say about the effects of childhood and adulthood?

   b In what ways could both poems be viewed as warnings?

   c What different techniques do they use to convey their message?

   d Which do you think is more effective?

Growing Up U. A. Fanthorpe

Content and theme

1 **Growing Up** gives an adult's view of the poet's own childhood. What sort of view is created by your first reading?

Imagery

2 Brainstorm the *images* below and explain how they show the poet's attitudes to herself, to others, and to the process of growing up.

- the long yawn of infancy
- Shoplifting daintily into my pram
- hairy, fleshy growths and monthly outbursts
- a criminal/Guilty of puberty
- Struggled to die on her feet / Never told anyone anything
- the natives' art of life
- wormed along years
- well-oiled bolts . . . slot into the grooves / Their ancestors smoothed out

Extension

Find out about Emily Brontë. What does such a choice of 'hero' tell us about the poet?

Language

3 The poem uses a lot of negative terms to describe growing up. See how many you can find to add to this list:

- sabotaging • despised • distrusted • criminal...

What is the combined effect of these?

4 Now look at the words Fanthorpe uses to describe others. How does the poet convey a sense of her own superiority?

Structure

5 How does the *structure* of the poem reflect the process of growing up?

6 What is the effect of repeating 'I wasn't good'?

Exploring your own response

7 Is this poet really saying she wasn't good, or is she implying she was something different and better? What qualities does she value in herself? If they didn't make her a good child, what did they make her good at?

Compare

- Compare **Growing Up** with another poem which offers a complicated or negative view of childhood (e.g. **I Remember, I Remember**).
- Which of the other poems presents a message from adults to children? Which do you think is the most effective?

West Pathway Steve Ellis

1 This short poem gives some very brief advice. With a partner, brainstorm the poem and consider the following questions.

a What do you think the poet means?

b Why would giving advice take 'guts'?

c What does living 'in a cul-de-sac' mean?

d Could this be a bitter comment on the poet's own life? Or a celebration?

The 1914–18 War was also known as the Great War, and is infamous for the millions of young men who died, using old-fashioned battle tactics against the first modern weapons, such as machine-guns. Young men volunteered to go and fight, believing they were on a heroic mission.

The horror they faced when they got to the trenches is the subject of much of their poetry. The soldiers felt betrayed by those who had persuaded them to go and fight, and were desperate to show the reality of war.

1 Look at the pictures below. They were all produced during the war. What attitude or message does each one suggest?

2 In groups, read through the poems in Section F of **Opening Lines**. Which poems seem to offer a similar attitude or message to each picture? Create a chart to show your answer to this.

3 Are there any poems in the section which do not match any of the pictures? Why might there be no publicity material for these poems? Does this help you understand why some of the poems were written?

a

WHEN YOU KNOW YOU'RE NOT FORGOTTEN BY THE GIRL YOU CAN'T FORGET (3).

"Roses may fade," answered the maid, "Clouds may turn sunshine to gloom,
But in my heart, though we're apart, love for you ever will bloom.
Through weary years, through smiles and tears, you'll find me faithful and true;
Dear heart, you'll learn, when you return, that I'm still waiting for you."

b

"THE CHILD HE WILL NEVER SEE!"
From the painting by Gordon Browne, R.I.

c

"Daily Mail" WAR PICTURES

70. BRITISH INFANTRY PRACTISING AN ATTACK.   OFFICIAL PHOTOGRAPH, CROWN COPYRIGHT RESERVED.

d

67. LOYAL NORTH LANCS. REGIMENT CHEERING WHEN ORDERED TO THE TRENCHES.   OFFICIAL PHOTOGRAPH, CROWN COPYRIGHT RESERVED.

Breakfast W.W. Gibson

Content and theme

1. This poem describes an ordinary event – breakfast – in the trenches. Identify the details that suggest the ordinariness and the horror. What do you think the poet is trying to tell us about life in the trenches?

Language

2. Explain how the following words and phrases create a picture of everyday life.

> - a rasher to a loaf of bread
> - Hull United would beat Halifax
> - played full-back
> - Jimmy/Billy/Ginger
> - cursed

Imagery

3. **Breakfast** creates a short scene that conjures a picture in the reader's mind. How do you imagine the following? Where and how is sound and movement used?

> - We ate our breakfast lying on our backs
> - shells were screeching overhead
> - Ginger raised his head
> - . . . and dropt back dead

Structure

4. The two parts of the opening sentence are linked by the word 'Because'. Why do you think the poet has linked the eating of breakfast and the shelling into one sentence? What does it help to emphasise about the experience?

5. Why do you think the poet has inserted a semi-colon rather than a comma here?

> and took the bet; and dropt back dead

6. The poem is written in one *stanza* but is constructed in three parts within this.
   - Why do you think the poet has begun and ended with the same lines?
   - What is he saying about the experience of eating breakfast while being shelled?
   - How does the poem suggest the men react to Ginger's death?

Exploring your own response

7. What do we learn about life in the trenches from **Breakfast**?

8. How does this poem use mundane details to suggest the horror of war?

9. Why do you think Gibson wrote this poem, and how successful has he been?

Exposure Wilfred Owen

Content and theme

1 Look at the title of the poem. What different meanings does the word 'exposure' have? Use a dictionary or thesaurus to help you answer this.

2 How are the various meanings of the word 'exposure' represented in the whole poem?

Imagery

3 The poem is rich in visual and aural *images* that help the reader to imagine what it was like in the trenches. Brainstorm the images below – and any others you find interesting. Think about what they convey and how they work.

- merciless iced east winds that knive us
- mad gusts tugging on the wire
- ranks on shivering ranks of grey
- flights of bullets streak the silence
- air that shudders black with snow
- blossoms trickling . . . blackbird fusses
- our ghosts drag home
- the innocent mice
- puckering foreheads crisp
- their eyes are ice

Language

Owen uses words for their sound as well as their meaning. This is what makes his poems as rich to listen to as to visualise.

4 Find examples of *onomatopoeia* and *assonance* used to create
- the sounds of trench warfare
- the sounds of the winter night
- the sounds of the men.

5 Owen uses assonance and *consonance* at the ends of lines. This helps bind the poem together, but creates a more uneasy feeling than full rhyme, which is appropriate for this poem. Find examples of this and judge how effective you think it is.

Structure

6 The poem is structured into eight *stanzas*. How does this division show the passage of time and change the focus?

7 Look at the final line of each stanza. Why do you think it is shorter?

8 What is the effect of the *repetition* of 'But nothing happens'?

9 What is the effect of the questions?

Exploring our own response

10 What do we learn about life in the trenches from **Exposure**?

⇄ **Compare**

Compare the poem's purpose and the poet's techniques with those in **Breakfast**.

Returning, We Hear the Larks Isaac Rosenberg

and The Dug-Out Siegfried Sassoon

Content and theme

1 These poems show us how close to death the young soldiers were, and how this led them to fear ordinary things. What sparks off their fear in each poem and why?

Imagery and Language

2 Both poems contain some striking *images*, which help to convey the moment and the emotions felt. Both poets use sound to create an aural impression of the events they describe. Brainstorm the images and phrases below to explore their effects.

Returning, We Hear the Larks	The Dug-Out
• sinister threat lurks • Dragging these anguished limbs • poison-blasted track • joy – joy – strange joy • Music showering our upturned list'ning faces • Death could drop from the dark • Like a blind man's . . . tides • kisses where a serpent hides	• legs ungainly huddled • one arm bent across … sullen, cold,/Exhausted face • Deep-shadow'd • candles guttering gold • mumble and sigh • *fall asleep for ever*

3 **Returning** contains some high-flown, poetic language, such as:

> • 'Sombre the night is'   • 'But hark!'   • 'Lo!'

How does this help to suggest the emotion in the poem?

4 **The Dug-Out** is written as if the poet is addressing the sleeping man.

   a What sort of question does it open with?
   b What does 'you wonder why' suggest?
   c Why does the poet try to shake his friend awake?
   d Why do you think the last two lines are in italics?

Structure

5 **Returning** is written in four *stanzas*. What does each stanza tell you?

6 **The Dug-Out** is written as a single stanza. How does the poet use punctuation to vary pace and emphasis?

Exploring your own response

7 How do the poems convey the effect of trench life on the men's emotional state?

⇄ Compare

How does the emotional impact on the soldiers in **Exposure** and **Breakfast** differ?

Of the Great White War Thomas Burke

Content and theme

1 Why do you think this poem is called **Of the Great <u>White</u> War**? What point is the poet trying to make?

2 What suggests that the poet feels detached from the whole thing?

Imagery

3 Thomas Burke creates *images* of the old which make us despise them. Match the images below with the descriptive statements, then explore how the quoted words from the poem suggest these meanings.

Image	Description
• cried aloud in public places • mouthed fair phrases • the Supreme Sacrifice • turned to their account books • brought out the bottles of wine	• What matters most to them is profit • Don't go without their luxuries • Making a big show • Hypocritical – they don't believe what they are saying • Dressing an idea up in grand-sounding phrases to convince people

Language

4 The poet uses words that were commonly used during the war to make people believe in the importance of fighting, for example 'duty', 'honour' and 'sacrifice'.

   a Who are these words associated with?

   b Are we supposed to take them seriously?

   c How does the poet show his opinion of such ideas through the people he associates with them?

5 What does 'sent out' suggest about how much choice the young men had?

Structure

6 The poet creates similar sentence structures, which contain opposite ideas to describe the fates of the aged and the young. What does this help to emphasise?

7 Look at the pattern of the lines and the pauses. How does Burke use punctuation to create this pattern? How does it emphasise key ideas?

Exploring your own response

8 What attitude to war emerges from this poem? How does the poet convey his personal views?

⇄ **Compare**

Compare this poem with any of the previous four. How do these views of those left behind at home affect your impressions of the soldiers' experiences?

War Girls Jessie Pope

In 1914 it was very unusual for women to work outside the home. Having a job was definitely thought to be a masculine prerogative. This poem is about the work that many women undertook during the war while the men who usually did such jobs were away fighting.

Content and theme

1 Who do you think the poem is aimed at and what is it trying to do?

Language

2 Make a list of all the verbs used to describe the girls' actions, for example:

- speeds • drives • whistles

What sort of impression do these convey?

3 Now look at these descriptions of the girls and their qualities:

- Strong • sensible • fit • energy and knack
- canny mother-wit

What impression of femininity is suggested here? What sort of behaviour is valued?

Imagery

4 The poet creates a series of descriptive pictures of women performing jobs previously done by men. What is the overall impression created by these pictures?

5 How does this picture contrast with qualities traditionally associated with girls, their interests and proper place before the war, as suggested by the following:

- No longer caged and penned up
- a heart that's soft and warm
- They've no time for love and kisses

Structure

6 **War Girls** has a regular *rhythm* and *rhyme scheme* – it sounds like a song.
   a How would you describe the mood of the poem?
   b How do the rhythm and rhyme scheme help to create this?
   c Why is it suitable for the poem's purpose?

Compare

Compare **War Girls** with the view of those at home in **Of the Great White War.**

Exploring your own response

7 Justify the following statements with evidence from the poem.
   a This poem tries to keep morale high during the war.
   b Women can work and stay feminine.
   c It is women's duty to stay cheerful and not grumble.
   d Women owe it to their absent men to work.
   e War is more important than love.

When you see millions . . . C. H. Sorley
and **Base Details** Siegfried Sassoon

Content and theme

1 Both poems suggest attitudes towards those who die in war. Try to decide on the purpose and audience for each poem. What attitudes are expressed or criticised?

Imagery

2 The poems create vivid visual *images* to help convey their message. Brainstorm the images and explain what they suggest to you and how they work.

Base Details	When you see . . .
• fierce, and bald, and short of breath • speed glum heroes • Guzzling and gulping • toddle safely home • die – in bed	• the mouthless dead • Across your dreams in pale battalions • each gashed head • the o'ercrowded mass • Great death . . . all his

Language

3 The language in each poem is used to create different effects. Find evidence from each poem to support the following statements.

 a In **When you see . . .** the sounds are mainly soft and haunting. In **Base Details** they are quick and clipped and angry.

 b **Base Details** uses *colloquial*, everyday language to express the view of a footsoldier. **When you see . . .** uses highly poetic language to express ideas about generations of the dead.

4 Both poets use *dialogue*, or *direct speech*.

 a Why have they done this?

 b How does it make the ideas/feelings more immediate?

Structure

5 **Base Details** has a strong and regular *rhythm* and a clear pattern of *rhyme*. How does this help create the mood?

6 The poem is written in *iambic pentameter*, a *metre* which closely resembles the rhythm of natural speech. Why is this suitable for this poem?

7 In what ways is **When you see . . .** a typical *sonnet*?

8 How does the poet use punctuation for dramatic effect when reading?

⇄ **Compare**

Compare attitudes to war and fighting in these poems with **Of the Great White War** and **War Girls**.

In Time of War Lesbia Thanet

Content and theme

1 This poem is about a woman's immature ideas about love and war, and then her recognition of the reality. How are these different ideas portrayed in the poem?

Imagery

2 Brainstorm the following *images* and explain how they support the ideas above.

- love past all romance
- heroes' women
- When the deep drums awake
- Go forth: do gloriously

- blind with fear
- lover made of dreams
- so commonplace, so dear
- knit with all I am or do

Language

3 The language in this poem varies from the high-flown and poetic to the simple and everyday.

  a Which *stanza* uses which type of language?
  b Identify examples of both types of language.
  c How does this contrast in language reinforce the key ideas in the poem?

Structure

4 The poem is written in two stanzas. Why do you think the poet done this?

5 Find quotations from the poem which express these contrasts:

- then and now
- dream man and real man
- glory and fear.

6 The final line of each stanza is written as a prayer:

- Go forth: do gloriously for my dear sake.
- Only God bring you back – God bring you back!

  a What are the differences in the two lines? What is emphasised by these?
  b What is the effect of the *repetition* of 'God bring you back' in the final line?

Exploring your own response

7 What does this poem suggest the speaker and women generally learned as a result of the war? How is this conveyed?

Compare

- Compare contrasting attitudes in **In Time of War** with **War Girls** and **Of the Great White War.**
- Compare the impact of war on women in **In Time of War** with **Sonnet.**

Sonnet Edna St Vincent Millay

Content and theme

1 From whose point of view is this poem written? How would you describe the mood? When do you think it might have been written in relation to the war?

Imagery

2 The poem contains some haunting *images*. Brainstorm those given below, using the Glossary to help you identify the techniques used. You could also draw what they convey, or find pictures that express the same ideas or feelings.

- what arms have lain / Under my head till morning
- the rain / Is full of ghosts tonight, that tap and sigh / Upon the glass
- turn to me at midnight with a cry
- in the winter stands the lonely tree
- birds have vanished one by one
- that summer sang in me

Language

3 The use of *rhyme* in this poem helps to maintain flow and unity, and also to create the mood of haunting sadness. Looks at these paired rhymes and consider the effect of the words together:

- why/sigh/reply/cry
- lain/rain/pain/again
- lonely tree/sang in me
- one by one/come and gone
- before/no more

Compare

- Compare contrasting attitudes in **Sonnet** with **War Girls** and **In the Great White War.**
- Compare the impact of war on women in **Sonnet** and **In Time of War**

Structure

4 Identify the features that make this poem a *sonnet*. How far do the ideas in this poem reflect those traditionally found in a sonnet?

5 How does the use of sound and punctuation in this poem help to create a suitable *rhythm* and pace for the subject?

Exploring your own response

6 What effects of war are conveyed in this poem?

7 What techniques does the poet use to convey her ideas. How successful is she?

Easter Monday Eleanor Farjeon

and At the Movies Florence Ripley Mastin

Content and theme

1 Both poems show us some of the effects of war on women. What are the feelings suggested in each? To whom is each poem addressed? Which is most personal?

Imagery

2 **At the Movies** offers some striking visual *images*. Match the images below to the descriptions, and brainstorm their effects.

Image	Description
• swing across the screen in brave array • grinding the dark grass • marched into the grey/Of battle • One lifts his dusty cap; his hair is bright • I meet his eyes • quivers into ghostly white	• suggestion of death • individual among the masses • pride and energy • a sense of personal connection • disappearing beyond sight • suggestion of killing nature

3 In **Easter Monday** the poet imagines the soldier getting the present. Find examples which help to create a sense of her care for the soldier as an individual.

4 How does the poet use a letter to make it vivid?

5 What is the effect of these images:

> • This is the eve   • our earliest seeds   • The apple-bud

Language

6 What effect does the use of the second person ('you') and quotations from the letter have in **Easter Monday**?

7 How does the use of *rhyme* help to achieve contrast in **At the Movies**?

Structure

8 Both these poems are structured in two parts. Why do you think each poet has done this? How does the focus change in the second *stanza* in each?

9 In **Easter Monday** the poet repeats key words and phrases in both stanzas to achieve contrast of expectation and reality. How does this help build up the drama and the sense of loss in the last line?

Exploring your own response

10 How does each poem convey a sense of individual loss? What do they add to your understanding of the women's perspectives?

Compare

Compare **Easter Monday** and **At the Movies** with **Sonnet** and **In Time of War**.

Disabled Wilfred Owen

Content and theme

1 Read through the poem. What is Owen telling us about the lives of injured war veterans?
   a Why did the young man join?
   b What is he missing out on?
   c What is his life like now?

2 How would you describe the mood of this poem?

Imagery

3 Brainstorm the *images* given below. Add any others you find striking or interesting.

- Legless, sewn short at elbow
- Voices of boys rang saddening like a hymn
- glow-lamps budded in the light blue trees
- how warm their subtle hands
- He's lost his colour

- purple spurted from his thigh
- Smiling they wrote his lie
- He thought of jewelled hilts
- drafted out with drums and cheers
- the women's eyes/Passed from him

4 How does Owen create images that appeal to different senses?

Language

5 Find examples in the poem of:

- sound   •   *repetition*   •   dramatic language.

Discuss their effects.

6 How do these phrases suggest the soldier's thoughts? What feelings are conveyed?

- Voices of play and pleasure after day
- Aye, that was it
- giddy jilts
- Why don't they come?

Structure

7 The poem is written in an uneven pattern of *stanzas*. How does the focus of each stanza shift? What links the first and last?

Exploring your own response

8 What does Owen suggest were the young soldier's motives for joining up?

9 This is a bitter and haunting poem. How are the following emotions presented?

- suffering   •   regret   •   blame.

10 What does Owen suggest is the soldier's reward for serving?

Compare

- Compare critical attitudes to jingoism (mindless ideas about patriotism used to get people to volunteer) in **Disabled, Of the Great White War** and **When you see millions of the mouthless dead.**

- Compare contrasting attitudes in **Disabled** and **War Girls**.

As the Team's Head-Brass Edward Thomas

Content and theme

1 The poem focuses on a key moment in time which makes a strong impression on the poet. Describe the events in the poem and the mood and feelings created.

Imagery

2 The poem creates a vivid picture of a country scene. Find and brainstorm *images* which convey details of the setting and the passing of time and the seasons.

3 What do you think the lovers might represent to the young man? Might this form part of the reason he has not joined up?

Language

4 Why do you think Thomas uses *dialogue* rather than just the poet's thoughts?

5 What is the effect of the ploughman's short answers?

6 How is the conversation used to suggest the effect of war on small communities?

7 How does the poet use dialogue to suggest a feeling of trust that the war is for good reasons?

8 The conversation clearly has an effect on the poet. What do you think he did next? (Look at the date of his death for a clue.) Why do you think this moment might have had such an effect on him?

Structure

9 How is *enjambment* and punctuation used to create flow in the poem?

10 How do the sentences echo the movement of the plough?

11 How is the mention of the lovers used to mark the time passing?

Exploring your own response

12 Discuss how far these statements might be true of the poem. Give evidence from the poem to back up your opinions.

a This is an idealised picture of the English countryside, which conveys what the soldiers were fighting for.

b This poem describes the effects of the loss of men on their friends and communities.

c Talking to the ploughman makes the poet feel it is his duty to join up.

d The beauty of nature and the young lovers remind us what young men's lives should be about.

 Compare

Compare views on the effects of war with **Sonnet** and **In Time of War**.

There will come soft rains . . . Sara Teasdale

and **Mental Cases** Wilfred Owen

Content and theme

1 Both of these poems describe the after-effects of war, but with strongly contrasting focus and *imagery*. Read through the poems and then summarise the effects and the poets' attitudes to war.

Imagery

2 Brainstorm these *images* from the two poems, and any others you find interesting.

There will come soft rains . . .	Mental Cases
• swallows calling with their shimmering sound • feathery fire • Whistling their whims • Spring herself, when she woke at dawn	• leer like skulls' teeth • Memory fingers in their hair of murders • Multitudinous murders • Dawn breaks open like a wound that bleeds afresh

3 Can you find examples of similar techniques used to create very different images?

Language

4 Find all the examples that you can in **There will come . . .** of words conveying:
   • soft sounds
   • colour/beauty
   • the five senses.

5 Find all the examples that you can in **Mental Cases** of words conveying:
   • harsh sounds
   • violence
   • death.

6 How do both poems create pictures of a world after war? How are they imaginary?

Structure

7 Compare the *rhythm* and pace created in each poem.
   a How would you describe the effects achieved?
   b How do they help create the mood?
   c How are they suited to the subject matter?

Exploring your own response

8 Both poets have a message about the effects of war.
   a What is the message in each and how successfully is it conveyed?
   b What contrasting ideas about the effects of war on nature, and the effects of war on people, can you find?

 Compare

• Compare the realities of war in **Mental Cases**, **Disabled** and **Exposure**.

• Compare ideas about rural England in **There will come . . .**, **As the Team's Head-Brass** and **Sonnet**.

Overview

Men and Women

To help you to explore links and contrasts between poems, and focus on techniques used to express ideas.

1 Find pairs of poems which show different views and feelings about the following ideas:

- being in love
- whether men or women are fickle
- whether women should marry
- why women are admired
- whether women should sleep with their lovers
- breaking up
- death of a lover.

2 Now, for each poem:

a Summarise the view and feelings.

b Give three ways in which these are conveyed to the reader. You *must* include at least *two* different techniques, and offer quotations to support your answers.

c Say which view you most understand and agree with.

An example is given below on the theme of why women are admired.

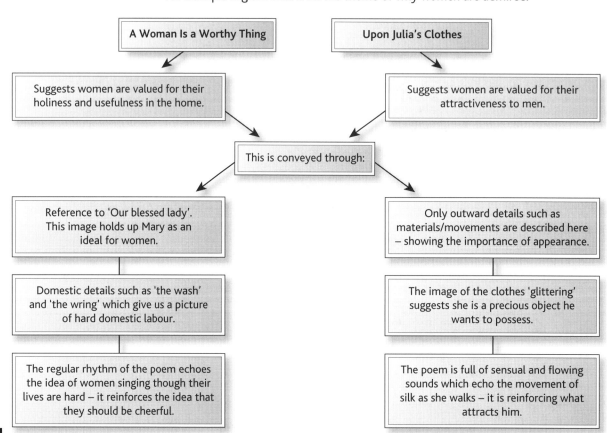

A Woman Is a Worthy Thing	Upon Julia's Clothes
Suggests women are valued for their holiness and usefulness in the home.	Suggests women are valued for their attractiveness to men.

This is conveyed through:

Reference to 'Our blessed lady'. This image holds up Mary as an ideal for women.	Only outward details such as materials/movements are described here – showing the importance of appearance.
Domestic details such as 'the wash' and 'the wring' which give us a picture of hard domestic labour.	The image of the clothes 'glittering' suggests she is a precious object he wants to possess.
The regular rhythm of the poem echoes the idea of women singing though their lives are hard – it reinforces the idea that they should be cheerful.	The poem is full of sensual and flowing sounds which echo the movement of silk as she walks – it is reinforcing what attracts him.

Time and Change

To help you develop your planning and reflection, as well as exploring links and contrasts between poems.

1 Choose two poems from this section, which illustrate one of the following themes:
- regret or nostalgia for the past
- changes from childhood to adulthood
- being haunted by the past
- human nature doesn't change
- the contrast between past and present
- changes in relationships.

2 Then copy and complete the planning map below.

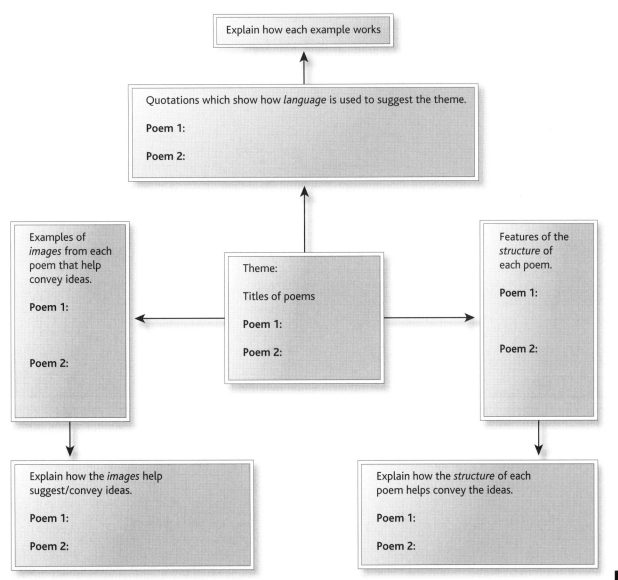

Explain how each example works

Quotations which show how *language* is used to suggest the theme.

Poem 1:

Poem 2:

Examples of *images* from each poem that help convey ideas.

Poem 1:

Poem 2:

Theme:

Titles of poems

Poem 1:

Poem 2:

Features of the *structure* of each poem.

Poem 1:

Poem 2:

Explain how the *images* help suggest/convey ideas.

Poem 1:

Poem 2:

Explain how the *structure* of each poem helps convey the ideas.

Poem 1:

Poem 2:

Generations

To help you develop your personal response to the poems and your skills in evaluation. You will decide which poems should stay in a Big Brother poetry house. Work through the flow diagram below.

You decide

You can do this alone or in pairs/groups. The idea is to be able to justify your decision with supporting evidence from the poem.

Which poem should stay if we judge by:

a Best creation of family life?
b Most striking images?
c Best creation of adult/child conflict?
d Best use of structure?
e Most interesting use of language?

Your nominations for each category:

1
2
3
4
5

For each nomination you must:

a Give your reason.

b Provide supporting quotation.

Discuss your ideas for 'Poems in the Big Brother house' with a partner and then present your ideas to the class.

The 1914–18 War [i]

To help develop your familiarity with the poems and the sorts of comments you will want to make in your own writing.

Look at the items below and match up the quotation to the poem and the idea. When you have finished, create more of your own to test your classmates.

No longer caged and penned up

This suggests the trust ordinary people had to have that the war was a good thing though they didn't understand.

The Dug-Out

Exposure

This image conveys the quality of old black and white film, and suggests the death of the young man / becoming a spirit

This suggests the innocence of people before the war, playing with ideas of patriotism.

your sullen, cold/Exhausted face

War Girls

ranks on shivering ranks of grey

This is a shocking image that shows young men laughing and as pieces of meat.

Treading blood from lungs that had loved laughter

At the Movies

In Time of War

God pity babes at play

As the Team's Head-Brass

This suggests that before the war womens' lives were limited – they are like trapped animals.

This suggests the sheer numbers of soldiers – they seem like a depersonalised suffering mass.

Mental Cases

The picture quivers into ghostly white

The three adjectives in this description suggest the suffering of the young men and the effect it is having on their spirits/mood.

If we could see all all might seem good

Poetry for examination in 2006–2008

War

OPENING LINES

This section deals with war poetry written *before* 1914. Because the numbers killed in the 1914–18 war (First World War) were so enormous people began to question the validity and morality of war on such a vast scale. Prior to 1914, attitudes towards patriotism, bravery and honour were more straightforward, although many poems in this section have a strong anti-war theme. Some are written about specific wars, as listed below:

Napoleonic Wars 1803–15   **Crimean War** 1854–56   **Boer War** 1899–1902

The Charge of the Light Brigade refers to the Battle of Balaclava in 1854 in the Crimean War.

On Lieutenant Eyre's Narrative... is about the Afghan Wars, the first of which was in 1839.

Verse Inviting Mrs C– to Tea on a public Fast-day ... is set in the American War of Independence, which began in 1776.

After Blenheim refers to the Battle of Blenheim in 1704, part of the War of the Spanish Succession.

'Come up from the fields father ...' refers to the American Civil War 1861–65.

The Destruction of Sennacherib is a battle mentioned in the Old Testament.

To Lucasta ... refers to the English Civil War 1642–88.

Ode, Written in the Beginning of the Year 1746. At the Battle of Culloden in 1746 the Jacobite rebellion was crushed by the Duke of Cumberland.

Attitudes to war

Before you read this section in **Opening Lines** it might be useful to think about your own attitudes to war and the attitudes found in books and in the media. Think about war films and television programmes you have seen. Are these set in pre-1914 wars, like *Sharp* or *Hornblower* on television, or in more modern wars, as in the films *Saving Private Ryan*, *Pearl Harbor* or *Forrest Gump*?

Discuss the following questions and statements with a partner:

a Is war always wrong?
b Would you join the armed forces voluntarily?
c If you were called up to fight in a war, would you go?
d What qualities does a soldier need?
e Would you fight to defend your country from invasion?
f Is it right to invade someone else's country?
g Is it right to fight a war against terrorism?
h Are some wars more justifiable than others?
i The old should not send young people off to die.
j Women should be allowed to fight on the front line.
k Wars in the past were very different to modern wars.

The Charge of the Light Brigade Alfred, Lord Tennyson

Content and theme

This poem was written about an event at the battle of Balaclava, where the Light Brigade charged towards the Russian cannons because they had been given the wrong order by mistake. While studying the poem, keep in mind what the poem tells you about Tennyson's attitude towards this event.

1 Find a key line from each of *stanzas* I to V, which tells you what actually happened in the charge.

2 Find a key line from stanza VI which shows how Tennyson wants you to respond.

Imagery

3 Look at some of the following *images* and examine how they convey the danger and destruction of the charge:

- the valley of Death
- Stormed at with shot and shell
- Into the jaws of Death
- Into the mouth of Hell
- Shattered and sundered

4 Do you think Tennyson thought that the charge was brave or foolhardy?

Language

5 What is the effect of using speech in stanzas I and II?

6 Find examples of *rhetorical* questions in stanzas II and VI. Are there any differences between the two rhetorical questions he asks?

Structure

7 The *rhythm* in the poem varies but Tennyson often uses one strong, followed by two weak beats (dum de dee). In what ways does this driving rhythm help you to visualise the scene?

8 Look at the lines below with a partner and decide on how many repetitions there are and why Tennyson repeats those lines.

- Into the valley of Death / Rode the six hundred
- Cannon to right of them, / Cannon to left of them

9 What effect does Tennyson create by the following *rhymes*:

- Their's not to make reply,
  Their's not to reason why,
  Their's but to do and die:
- Stormed at with shot and shell,
  While horse and hero fell,
  They that had fought so well

Exploring your own response

10 Do you agree with Tennyson that we should 'Honour the charge they made' or has some of the imagery in the poem made you feel differently?

The Volunteer Herbert Asquith

Content and theme

The oriflamme was the sacred banner of St Denis, made of red silk, which was taken into battle by French kings. It has come to symbolise any rallying point in a struggle.

1 The poem is about a young man who volunteers to go off to war. Find quotations from the poem which show that:

- he never expected to go to war
- he dies in the war
- he dreamed of heroism
- the poet considers his death to be heroic.

2 Unlike Tennyson's poem, this one is about one person. What is your impression of the volunteer's character and how has this been created?

Imagery

3 In the first *stanza*, the clerk's ordinary life is contrasted with the glamour of battle. Explain how the following images contrast:

- city grey/the gleaming eagles
- no lance broken in life's tournament/Went thundering past beneath the oriflamme.

4 In the second stanza, his death is described using *images* of time. How does the poet soften the effect of his death by writing: 'From twilight to the halls of dawn he went'?

Language

Extension

In the last line the poet refers to the Battle of Agincourt. This links the volunteer with the national heroes who beat the French in 1415.

- Research Henry's Agincourt speech by Shakespeare in *King Henry V*, Act IV scene III.
- What impression of the volunteer and his place in history is Asquith giving by this reference to Agincourt?

5 Asquith uses some of the same techniques as Tennyson, such as *alliteration*. Why do you think he uses alliteration in the following lines?

- Thinking that so his days would drift away
- Yet ever 'twixt the books and his bright eyes

Structure

6 The *rhythm* of Line 11 is broken up by a semi-colon in the middle of the line:

His lance is broken; but he lies content

Why do you think Asquith chose to do this?

7 He rhymes 'went' and 'content', 'recompense' and 'hence' and 'last resort' and 'Agincourt' in the second stanza. What is the effect of linking these words?

Exploring your own response

8 In what way does the language of the poem make the volunteer's death seem heroic?

9 **The Volunteer** does not use any details of battle at all. How does this affect your response to the poem, compared to your reaction to the **Light Brigade**?

On Lieutenant Eyre's Narrative . . . Thomas Hood
and **Verses Inviting Mrs. C – to Tea . . .** Anna Seward

These two poems criticise war by using humour. Although they take a different attitude, particularly in their approach to heroism and honour, they use similar techniques to the other poets. Here is some information to help you with **Verses Inviting . . . .**

Structure
The first half of the poem is in mock-letter form, inviting 'Stella' to break the public fast. The fast is being held in order to 'please the Lord' and to enable American throats to be 'cut . . . at will'.

The second half of the poem supports the fast by explaining that the American War of Independence has been sparked off by the tax on tea, commencing at the Boston Tea Party where a ship's cargo of tea was poured into Boston Harbour.

Style
Mock-heroic: something very ordinary (like tea) is written about in flowery, poetic language, often with references to Greek and Roman mythology.

References
Ate was the daughter of Zeus in Greek mythology. She led both men and gods into rash and impulsive actions. Atreus and Thyestes were brothers. After a family history of murder and mayhem, Atreus murdered Thyestes's sons and served them up to him at a banquet. The house was thereafter cursed with famine. Phoebus is the sun god.

1 Use the bullet points in the chart below to help you explore how these two poems create their comic and critical effects.

On Lieutenant Eyre's Narrative . . .	Verses Inviting . . .
• Use of *alliteration* • Use of *rhyme* • Use of *repetition* • Works in a similar way to a joke • Very brief	• Use of *mock-heroic* • Amusing descriptions of tea • Use of alliteration for comedy • Use of classical references • Use of *rhyming couplets* • Use of strong four beat *rhythm* • Use of violent *imagery*

Exploring your own response

2 Are **On Lieutenant Eyre's Narrative** and **Verses Inviting . . .** merely entertaining or do they have a serious point to make about war?

⇄ Compare
• How does the structure of **Verses Inviting . . .** differ from that of **The Volunteer** and **The Charge of the Light Brigade**? What is the effect of these differences?

• The **Volunteer** uses references to Roman soldiers and the Battle of Agincourt. How are they used differently to the classical references in **Verses Inviting . . .**?

After Blenheim Robert Southey

Content and theme

After Blenheim is a *narrative* poem – a poem which tells a story.

1. Write about six sentences which summarise the story of the poem.

2. What role do the children Wilhelmine and Peterkin play in the poem?

3. Which of their questions is their grandfather, old Kaspar, unable to answer?

Imagery

4. Look at *stanzas* VII, VIII and IX. What impressions of war are created by the *images* in these stanzas?

Language

5. Which words help to convey the innocence of the children in the poem?

6. How does Southey use *alliteration* in stanzas VII, VIII and IX to emphasise the effects of war?

Structure

7. What is the effect of using speech in the poem?

8. The poet repeats 'famous victory' in several different ways in the poem. What is the effect of this? (Remember: politicians are taught to use *repetition* when they want to question or cast doubt on an opponent's policy.) How is Southey questioning the 'famous victory' idea here?

9. Why do you think Southey uses *rhyming couplets* to end each stanza?

10. How do these couplets reinforce the effect of repeating 'famous victory' towards the end of the poem?

Exploring your own response

11. It is a common saying that truth comes 'out of the mouths of babes . . .' How do the children in the poem affect your view of war?

12. Do you think it is true that the older generation are more fatalistic and accepting of war than the younger?

13. What do you think the poem is saying about war leaders and famous victories?

The Drum John Scott

Content and theme

1 Unlike **After Blenheim**, where the message is not immediate, John Scott makes his feelings about war very clear. How does he achieve this in the first line?

2 In the first stanza, what does the poet say the drum means to 'thoughtless youth'?

3 In the second stanza, what does he say it means to him?

Imagery

4 Scott personifies the drum itself and Ambition in the first stanza and Misery in the second stanza. What does the use of *personification* add to the poem?

5 If you had to draw Ambition and Misery, as personified in this poem, what sort of pictures would you create?

6 What *image* of war is created in the second stanza?

7 What similarities do these images have in common with those in **After Blenheim**?

Language

8 Why do you think the poet chose to use the following words in the poem?

• discordant	• tawdry	• mangled	• lures
• Parading	• glittering	• catalogue	• ravaged

9 What is the effect of the *alliteration* used in lines 3 and 8?

10 In what ways does the poet use *assonance* in the rhymes of the second stanza?

Structure

11 How does the use of *repetition* in the poem fit in with its subject – the drum?

12 The poem generally has a regular *rhythm* – why?

13 What is the effect of making the final line in each stanza longer (five strong beats, rather than four)?

Exploring your own response

14 Which of the following points added most to your enjoyment of the poem:

- its rhythm
- its use of *rhyming couplets*
- its directness
- its use of repetition
- its use of a drum as a symbol of war
- other aspects of the poem?

⇄ Compare

Which of the two poems, **After Blenheim** and **The Drum,** do you think conveys the poet's views on war more effectively?

The Hyaenas Rudyard Kipling
and Tommy's Dead Sydney Dobell

These two poems follow on well from **After Blenheim** and **The Drum** because they are also concerned with the war dead and the aftermath of battle. As in the previous two poems, you are going to look at how the poet's attitudes to war are conveyed through imagery, language and structure.

Imagery and language

1 Copy and complete the chart below to note down the relevant evidence from the two poems.

Technique	The Hyaenas	Tommy's Dead
Comparison		
Words which suggest sympathy for victims		
Alliteration	'They snout the bushes and stones aside'	
Onomatopoeia		
Repetition		
Images of a ruined land where nothing will grow		'The hills are wizen and thin'
Lists		
Speech		
Imagery of the natural world		

2 Make a note of all the images of the natural world from **After Blenheim, The Drum, The Hyaenas, Tommy's Dead.** In what ways do all four poems use the natural world to make their point about war?

Exploring your own response

3 How do **The Hyaenas** and **Tommy's Dead** affect your feelings about war?

4 Which aspects of the four poems you looked at in question 2 had the most powerful effect on you and why?

'Vitaï Lampada' means 'beacon of life' and refers to the school motto 'Play up, play up and play the game'.

Vitaï Lampada Henry Newbolt

Content and theme

1. What is your school motto? What values does it promote?

2. The poem is about a schoolboy initially. What sort of schoolboy is he and what sort of school would he have attended at the time the poem was written?

3. What situation is established in the first stanza? How does the situation in the second stanza differ? What are the similarities between the two situations?

4. In what ways does the third stanza draw the themes of the poem together?

Imagery

5. Look at Newbolt's use of *imagery*.

   a In line 7, why do you think he uses the word 'smote'?

   b In line 13, what is conveyed by 'The river of death has brimmed his banks'?

   c In line 22, what is suggested by the simile 'like a torch in flame'?

Language

6. How does Newbolt create tension from the very first line of the poem?

7. 'A bumping pitch and a blinding light' literally describes the batsman's predicament but what parallels are there with all difficult situations?

8. How do lines 5 and 6 give a moral view of why the batsman should play well? What key words in these two lines does Newbolt link by *alliteration*?

9. What specifically military language does Newbolt use in the second stanza? How do these terms place the poem firmly in the nineteenth century?

10. Why do you think he chose the words 'dare' in line 20 and 'joyful' in line 21?

Structure

11. In what ways does the poet use *repetition* to develop the theme of the poem through the three stanzas?

12. How does the *rhyme* and *rhythm* of the poem add tension and pace?

Exploring your own response

13. Which of these views of the poem comes closest to your own?

    a It has outdated values of bravery and honour.

    b It is a dramatic and moving poem.

    c It makes light of sacrificing young men in war.

    d You cannot compare sport and war.

    e The values you learn at school can be essential in later life.

14. You can enjoy a poem even if you do not agree with the sentiments expressed in it. What did you find particularly interesting or effective about the poem?

The Man He Killed Thomas Hardy

Content and theme

1. This poem is a *dramatic monologue* – where a character speaks to an unseen and unheard audience. Who do you think the soldier is speaking to here and where do you imagine them to be?

2. What sort of soldier is the narrator of the poem?

3. How did the other man's death occur?

4. What do the two men have in common?

5. What does the last stanza suggest about the character of the speaker?

Language

6. Which words in the poem suggest that the speaker is an ordinary working man?

7. Why do you think Hardy chose to use the following words in the poem:

> • ancient   • nipperkin   • ranged   • off-hand   • quaint

Structure and form

8. Why do you think Hardy repeats 'foe' in stanza three?

9. In what other way is the third stanza different to the other stanzas?

10. What do you think the third stanza suggests about the speaker's feelings towards the man he killed?

11. What is the effect of using so many dashes in the fourth stanza?

Exploring your own response

12. This poem takes a more reflective and questioning approach to war than **Vitaï Lampada**. What questions about war is it asking?

13. How does the fact that we hear an individual's voice in this poem affect your reaction to it?

⇄ **Compare**

- How does the *rhythm* differ from that of **Vitaï Lampada**? What is the effect of this?
- What different purposes do you think Newbolt and Hardy had in writing these poems?

On the Idle Hill A. E. Housman and Song Anne Brontë

1 Use a chart like the one below to help you explore the similarities and differences between **On the Idle Hill** and **Vitaï Lampada**.

	On the Idle Hill	Vitaï Lampada
Content	Man goes off to war	Schoolboy grows up and goes off to war…
Openings		
Structure (plus *rhythm* and *rhyme scheme*)		
Use of contrast		
Use of language		
Attitudes to war		
Attitudes to courage and patriotism		

2 Which poet do you think has the more reflective and questioning attitude towards men going off to war? Remember to give reasons for your opinion.

3 Now look at **Song** compared to **The Man He Killed**. Use a chart like the one below to help you explore the similarities and differences between the two poems.

	Song	The Man He Killed
Use of contrast	'We have their princely homes and they / To our wild haunts …'	
Use of comparison		
Empathy with the enemy		
Use of *colloquial language*		'Right many a nipperkin!'
Imagery of the natural world		
Structure (verse and line length, rhythm and rhyme scheme)		
Mood and *tone*		

4 What do you think are the main similarities and differences between these two poems?

5 Which poem did you find the more moving – **Song** or **On the Idle Hill**?

Come up from the fields father . . . Walt Whitman

This is a dramatic poem in which a family receives the news that their son has been injured in war. Unknown to them, although the letter says that he will soon be better, the boy, Pete, is already dead by the time they receive it. Walt Whitman was an American poet, as you can see from the poem's setting in Ohio.

Content and theme

1. How does the poet set the scene?
2. How does the boy's mother react to the letter?
3. How do the daughters attempt to comfort her?
4. How does the mother react when she knows that her only son is dead?

Imagery

5. What picture of the farm and its surroundings is created in the first four *stanzas*?
6. How does this *image* of the farm and 'teeming and wealthy Ohio' contrast with the rest of the poem?

Language

7. How does the language used to depict the farm appeal to the senses of sight, sound and smell? (You will need to comment on *alliteration*, *assonance* and *onomatopoeia* here.)
8. Find examples of *repetition* of both single words and phrases in the poem (for example, 'Lo', 'all', 'is dead'). How do these repetitions add drama to the poem?
9. How is repetition used for different effects in lines 6–10 and lines 12–13?

Structure

10. What is the significance of the word 'But' in line 12 in the overall structure of the poem?
11. At what point in the poem does Whitman shift to the mother's perspective?
12. How do the following aspects of the poem add to the suspense and/or drama of the events in it?
    - the use of speech
    - the use of brackets
    - long lines
    - the listing technique in the final verse
    - short lines.

Exploring your own response

13. How does Whitman use *irony* in the poem?
14. How does he create sympathy for the characters in the poem? Look closely at the description of the mother in the poem as your starting point.
15. How does he use the natural world differently from Sydney Dobell in **Tommy's Dead**?
16. This poem says very little about war itself. Sum up the ways in which Whitman conveys his feelings about war to you.

Extension

Present a dramatic reading of the poem, using different voices for the narrator, the writer of the letter, and the daughter.

The Destruction of Sennacherib Lord Byron

Content and theme

1 How does the first *stanza* suggest the power of the Assyrian army?

2 What happens to them overnight? (second stanza)

3 Who is responsible for their destruction?

Imagery

4 One of the main figures of speech in this poem is *simile*. Examine the following similes and explain why they are appropriate. Make a chart like the one below to write out your explanations.

- like stars on the sea
- Like the leaves of the forest when Summer is green
- Like the leaves of the forest when Autumn hath blown
- And cold as the spray of the rock-beating surf
- like snow

Simile	Explanation
'like the wolf on the fold'	Like a wolf Sennacherib is fierce, predatory and powerful. A fold is a sheep pen. The sheep are powerless and vulnerable like the Israelites. The simile also suggests a surprise or ruthless element in the attack.

Language

5 Find three examples of *alliteration* in the poem and explain the effect in each case.

Structure

6 What is the effect of the *repetition* of 'and' at the beginnings of lines?

7 How does the use of *antithesis* in the second stanza suggest the power of the Angel of Death?

8 Do you think the *rhythm* and *rhyme scheme* are appropriate to the theme?

Exploring your own response

9 Looking back over the *imagery* and language of the poem, for example 'chill' 'gasping', 'distorted', would you say that it is a poem which glamorises war?

Byron's poem describes a biblical battle. Assyria was an ancient empire in Mesopotamia, roughly where Iraq is now. Sennacherib sent a threatening letter to Hezekiah, the King of Judah, who did not want to submit to Assyrian rule. He spread Sennacherib's letter out in the temple in Jerusalem. Later that night Isaiah, a prophet, relayed the Lord's encouraging message that his Angel of Death had visited Sennacherib's forces. The story is in 2 Kings 19:20–34.

⇄ **Compare**

Compare the description of suffering and grief in this poem with **Come up from the fields father . . .**

To Lucasta, Going to the Wars Richard Lovelace

and Ode . . . William Collins

These two poems take a contrasting approach to war compared to **Come up from the fields father . . .** and **The Destruction of Sennacherib**, even though the **Ode** has a similar theme. These poems suggest that it is brave and honourable to die in war.

1 Which of the two poems convinces you more effectively that war is honourable? Explain how each poet has achieved this effect. Use the notes in the chart below to help you answer.

 Compare

Choose two contrasting poems from **Come up from the fields father . . .**, **The Destruction of Sennacherib**, **To Lucasta . . .**, **Ode . . .**

Now compare the following:

• content
• structure
• use of language
• attitude to war
• impact on the reader.

To Lucasta	Ode . . .
• Who is the poet's new mistress? • Image for his relationship with Lucasta in stanza one? • *Metaphysical poem* – uses imagery which argues a case – how well? • Dramatic poem • Love for Lucasta would be invalid if he did not go to war. Why? • What would her reaction be?	• Key words which describe the dead? • *Personifies* Honour and Freedom – effect? • Supernatural element – moving? unrealistic? sentimental? • *Alliteration* – effect? • *Rhyme scheme* – effect? • The exclamation mark – effect? • No direct description of the dead. Makes it less powerful?

Town and Country

Before you read the poems in this section, think about the cycle of the seasons in Britain. Unlike other countries, where the weather is less variable, we have four distinct seasons.

1 Copy and complete the circle below and use it to brainstorm the things you associate with each season:

2 Now quickly look through Section D in **Opening Lines** and find the titles of poems which make references to the seasons. Add their titles to your chart.

3 Below are some quotations from the poems which refer to the seasons. Add them to your chart to give you an overview of the theme of changing seasons in the section:

- For thy delight each May morning
- To wayward Winter reckoning yields
- And shall she and I not go there once again now March is nigh
- Yet, if you enter the woods / Of a summer evening late
- The yellow leaves begin to fade
- Of the cowslip and primrose sweet
- And gathering swallows twitter in the skies

4 Now look at your chart and explore the kinds of ideas and feelings which you and the poets have connected to each season.

Some poets in the section write about the changing seasons and the beauty of the countryside, others look at the downside of living in the country. The same is true of the writing about towns. Some poets see towns as beautiful – others see them as places of hardship and oppression.

5 Find poems which fit into the following categories.
   a Country as a peaceful, beautiful place.
   b Country as a difficult place to live in.
   c Town as beautiful and picturesque place.
   d Town as a place of hardship and oppression.

Beeny Cliff Thomas Hardy

Content and theme

1. What kind of day is it, according to the first two *stanzas* of the poem?
2. How does the cloud in stanza III make the day seem even more beautiful?
3. What darker thought comes to Hardy in stanza IV?
4. Although the cliff still stands, what has happened to Hardy's wife?

Imagery

5. How does Hardy use *imagery* to suggest:
   - the beauty of the sea and the weather
   - the height of the cliff
   - an underlying sadness (in stanza III)
   - that the cliffs will always be there?

Language

6. There is a great deal of *alliteration* in the poem. Find some patterns of alliteration which help to suggest:
   - a blustery, windy day
   - the noise of the waves
   - the solidity of the cliff
   - the sunshine after the cloud
   - that the couple were in love.

7. How does the *assonance* in 'pale mews plained' add sound to the poem?

Structure

8. How does Hardy create a sense of joy and exhilaration through the *rhythm*?
9. Every line in each verse *rhymes*. What is the effect of the rhymes in each verse? How do the sounds of the rhymes in the last two verses fit in with the content of those verses?
10. Why do you think Hardy uses the word 'elsewhere' in line 14? Why does he place this word between dashes?
11. In what ways is the last line a sad contrast to the rest of the poem?

Exploring your own response

12. Explore the ways in which the poem suggests to you that:
    - the natural world is relatively permanent
    - human life is more fragile and transient (fleeting, of short duration).

13. What do you find moving in the poem?

On Wenlock Edge A. E. Housman

Content and theme

1. How is the storm which Housman observes similar to one in the past?
2. What did Housman and the Roman soldier have in common?
3. Where are the Roman and his troubles now?

Imagery

4. In the first *stanza* Housman personifies the wood, the Wrekin and the gale. How do these *personifications* suggest the power of the wind?
5. What is the effect of the image 'And thick on Severn snow the leaves'?
6. In the fourth stanza, Housman uses an *extended metaphor*. What is he suggesting by comparing life to a gale in line 14 and man to a tree in the gale in line 15?

Language

7. What effect do you think Housman wanted to create by using the following words?

   - threshed   • heaving   • in riot   • ashes

8. What is the effect of the *alliteration* in:

   - holt and hanger
   - forest fleece
   - heaving hill
   - wind … woods
   - Are ashes?

   Why might Housman have deliberately used the 'h', 'f' and 'w' sounds in particular?

Structure

9. Why does Housman use *antithesis* in line 16 of the poem?
10. What is the effect of Housman choosing a regular *rhyme* and *rhythm* scheme?

Exploring your own response

11. What do you think the poem is saying about:
    - the power of nature
    - human nature and human life
    - the relationship between humans and the natural world
    - the passing of time.

Sidebar notes:

Wenlock Edge is a high plateau in Shropshire, with wonderful views. The Wrekin is a small mountain which stands out from the rest of the countryside and is a local landmark. Uricon (Uriconium or Viroconium) is an old Roman settlement situated near the village of Wroxeter.

A high Roman wall still stands at the site. The River Severn runs through the county.

A holt is a wood or copse. A hanger is a wood on the side of a steep slope.

⇄ Compare

Identify the similarities and differences between this poem and **Beeny Cliff**. Consider the setting, verse form, content and theme, rhyme and rhythm, imagery, and what each poem has to say about the passing of time.

The Passionate Shepherd . . . Christopher Marlowe

and The Nymph's Reply . . . Sir Walter Ralegh

These two poems are unique in the section in that one is a reply to the other! Ralegh's poem *parodies* Marlowe's 'fairy tale' version of country life. Like Hardy in **Beeny Cliff** and Housman in **On Wenlock Edge**, Ralegh reflects on the fact that time passes and nothing human remains the same.

1 Explore the similarities and differences between these two poems in a chart like the one below.

	The Passionate Shepherd to His Love	The Nymph's Reply . . .
Depiction of nature		
Use of language	Fairy-tale elements – 'buckles of the purest gold'	
Imagery of the seasons		
Repetition		
Effect of time		'The flowers do fade'
Rhyme scheme		
Effect of rhyme scheme		
Use of *alliteration*		
Use of *antithesis*		

2 Which elements in Marlowe's poem would make you join the shepherd and which would put you off?

3 Do you think that Marlowe's poem deserved Ralegh's realistic, rather dark reply?

Imagery

4 **The Nymph's Reply . . .** and **On Wenlock Edge** concentrate on the harshness of nature. Find similar images from these two poems which prove this.

The Nymph's Reply	On Wenlock Edge
'Soon break, soon wither'	'But then it threshed another wood'

5 How is the imagery here different to that in **The Passionate Shepherd . . .**?

Exploring your own response

6 **The Passionate Shepherd to His Love** and **Beeny Cliff** are both love poems. Explore the ways in which these two poems treat the theme of love. Remember to include your own response to the ideas and feelings in the poems.

Composed Upon Westminster Bridge, September 3, 1802 William Wordsworth

> If you have visited the London Eye, you will have seen this poem displayed at its base. It does seem a good poem for a tourist attraction as Wordsworth was very impressed by his early morning view of London.

Content and theme

1 Find three aspects of the view which Wordsworth finds impressive.

2 Do you think he would have found London so beautiful if he had seen it later in the day?

3 Which aspects of the poem tell you that it is not a modern poem? (You could look at both the content and the language here.)

Imagery

4 What do you think Wordsworth means by saying the city wears the beauty of the morning 'like a garment'?

5 What does 'steep' mean in line 9? How does Wordsworth use this word metaphorically and to what effect?

6 Why is 'that mighty heart' a good *metaphor* for a city?

Language

7 Look at the following aspects of the poem and say what you think they contribute to its effect:

> - the words 'touching' and 'majesty' in line 3
> - the list in lines 5–6
> - the words 'bright' and 'glittering' in line 8
> - the *alliteration* in line 9
> - the *repetition* and use of commas in line 11
> - the *personification* of the River Thames
> - the exclamation 'Dear God!'

Structure

8 What are the typical features of a *sonnet*? Which type of sonnet is Wordsworth's poem? Decide how the poem is divided up. Look at the punctuation and the *rhyme scheme* to help you decide.

9 In a *sonnet* there is usually a change of some sort after the eighth line. What change do you notice here?

10 The poem is written in *iambic pentameter*. What does Wordsworth do to break up the *rhythm* of the lines? Where does he do this and why?

11 Sonnets are often love poems. In what ways is this like a love poem to the city?

Exploring your own response

12 This poem is in the BBC book *The Nation's Favourite Poems*. Why do you think it is so popular?

London William Blake

Content and theme

1. How does Blake describe the expressions on people's faces in the first stanza?
2. Why do you think he connects chimney sweepers with the church and the soldiers and the palace in the third stanza?

Imagery

There is some powerful *imagery* in the poem.

3. What image does 'mind-forged manacles' create in your mind? Who does Blake blame for the creation of these 'manacles'?
4. Why is the church described as 'blackening'?
5. How and why does Blake link the 'harlot's curse' in line 14 with the image 'marriage hearse' in line 16?
6. Some of the images are almost surreal, like the special effects in a film. In what ways are '. . . soldier's sigh/Runs in blood down palace walls' and 'marriage hearse' surreal?

Language

7. Blake uses much *repetition* in the poem. Analyse the effect of the repetition of the following words:

   - chartered
   - mark/s
   - In
   - Every

8. What is the impact of the *alliteration* on the letter 'b' in the final stanza: 'But/Blasts/blights'?
9. Which *rhymes* in the poem do you think:
   - create an appropriate sound
   - conclude the poem strongly and effectively
   - link key ideas.

Exploring your own response

10. Use some of the following words and phrases to explore Blake's attitude to the society described in the poem:
    - hypocrisy
    - corruption
    - bureaucratic laws
    - repression
    - oppression
    - child-labour.
    - poverty
    - cruelty
    - disease
    - responsibility

11. What is your response to the society he describes in the poem?

Extension

Which poem appeals to you more – Blake's or Wordsworth's? Write a speech which argues the case for your choice and present it to the class.

Compare

Compare the imagery in this poem to that in Wordsworth's **Composed Upon Westminster Bridge.**

Conveyancing Thomas Hood
and **Symphony in Yellow** Oscar Wilde

Conveyancing is a much more light-hearted poem than **London** or **Composed Upon Westminster Bridge**. It also contrasts with Wordsworth's poem in that it is about the busy traffic of the city and the hustle and bustle of London life.

Symphony in Yellow is like a painting with a strong use of colour and creation of a particular atmosphere. It also has a different mood and atmosphere compared to Wordsworth's poem.

1 Use the following notes to help you compare and contrast the two poems :

Conveyancing	Symphony in Yellow

• Title means carrying people from one place to another.
 	
• Many types of traffic/transport. What are they all?
 	
• *Structure* suggests intense activity – how?
 	
• Some pretty terrible *rhymes* – create humour.
 	
• Other jokes in the poem?
 	
• Use of italics – adds to comic effect.
 	
• Poet uses references to: *Shakespeare*:
  a Queen Mab – she appears in a speech by Mercutio in Shakespeare's *Romeo and Juliet* and is queen of the fairies.
  b 'the world a sage has call'd a stage' refers to Shakespeare's *As You Like It* – 'All the world's a stage and all the men and women merely players'
 	
• *Malthus* – a clergyman who was in favour of population control.
 	
• Totally comic – or serious issues too?
	• Why 'Symphony'?
	
	• Structure of the poem?
	
	• Effect of insect image in stanza I?
	
	• Look at the *similes* – which is the most effective?
	
	• Is he merely observing?
	
	• Is he creating a particular mood and atmosphere? How?
	
	• Why yellow?
	
	• Look at use of:
	  • *alliteration*
	  • *rhyme*
	  • *assonance*
	  • contrasting colour in the last line.
	
	• Very few people in the poem – effect?

Binsey Poplars Gerard Manley Hopkins

Content and theme

1 Hopkins's approach to the felling of the trees is quite modern in its concern for the environment. How is this concern outlined in the second *stanza* of the poem?

Imagery

2 The first stanza of the poem expresses Hopkins's feelings about the loss of the trees. How do these *images* convey his feelings?

- airy cages quelled
- Quelled or quenched in leaves the leaping sun
- Of a fresh and following folded rank
- dandled a sandalled/Shadow

The second stanza looks at the damage done to the environment.

3 Which image compares the countryside to a woman?

4 Which image compares it to an eye and in what way is this last image shocking?

Language

Hopkins liked to use *compound words* and to make up words and terms of his own.

5 What do you think the phrase 'wind-wandering/weed-winding' contributes to the effect of the first stanza?

6 What do you think Hopkins means by 'unselve' in line 22, a word he has made up?

7 Find examples of *alliteration* and *onomatopoeia*. How do these help you to see and hear the scene Hopkins is describing?

8 Why do you think Hopkins chose to use the following words in the poem:

- sleek
- delve
- havoc
- especial

Structure

9 Look at the shape the poem makes on the page. How does this fit its theme?

10 In what ways does Hopkins use *repetition* to convey his feelings about the trees?

11 Where does he use *rhyme* to emphasise particular words and ideas? (Some of the rhymes are internal – they rhyme within a line like 'hack' and 'rack'.)

Exploring your own response

12 What do you think of the last three lines of the poem? Are they sentimental?

13 How does Hopkins make the trees really individual and special in the poem?

To Autumn John Keats

Content and theme

1 Which aspects of autumn does Keats emphasise in each *stanza*?

2 How does the poem take you through:

- one autumn day
- the whole season of autumn
- different country settings?

Extension

Choose a different season and write either a description of it or a poem about it.

Use *personification*, *alliteration*, *onomatopoeia*, *simile* and *metaphor*.

Include the use of the senses in your writing.

If you are studying art at GCSE, find some paintings – such as winter scenes by Brueghel – to give you ideas. Can you find a painting to fit Keats's poem?

Imagery

3 Keats *personifies* autumn throughout the poem.

a What sort of 'person' is autumn in the first stanza?
b What is he doing in the second stanza?
c How does Keats praise him in the third stanza?

Language

4 Look at the way in which the poet creates the sights, sounds and textures of autumn. Use a highlighter pen to identify his use of *alliteration*, *assonance*, *onomatopoeia*. Use a different colour for each technique.

5 How does Keats suggest that autumn is an abundantly fruitful and ripe season? How do the verbs in the first stanza add to this impression of autumn as a great provider?

6 What words and techniques suggest the heat of midday in the second stanza?

7 How does Keats convey the sounds of autumn in the third stanza?

8 Select three examples of alliteration that you find effective. Give your reasons.

9 Select three onomatopoeic words from the poem and say why they are effective.

10 Keats uses three *rhetorical questions* in the poem. What is their effect on you?

Structure

11 The stanzas in the poem are long – eleven lines each. Why do you think Keats chose this number of lines rather than eight or ten?

12 He rhymes the seventh line with the eleventh line in each stanza. Why do you think he makes you wait for a concluding rhyme?

13 Find three run-on lines in the poem, for example, '… borne aloft/Or sinking'. What effect does Keats create with this use of *enjambment*?

Compare

What are the similarities and differences between this poem and **Binsey Poplars**?

Exploring your own response

14 How does the final stanza suggest that autumn is on its way out? What is the tone of this stanza and how does it make you feel?

The Way Through the Woods Rudyard Kipling
The Lake Isle of Innisfree William Butler Yeats
and **The Eagle** Alfred, Lord Tennyson

Content and theme

1 Look at how all three poets treat the theme of nature.
   a Do they concentrate on the beauty of nature or its power?
   b Do they introduce a supernatural element?
   c Are they more concerned with the poet's relationship with nature?

Imagery

2 Select six lines from the three poems which you think best describe the beauty of nature, such as the line below. Give reasons for your choice in each case.

> There midnight's all a glimmer, and noon a purple glow

Language

3 All three poems use a variety of poetic techniques. What techniques are being used in the quotations below and to what effect? Copy the chart and fill the gaps.

Quotation	Technique	Effect
bee-loud glade		
I hear lake water lapping with low sounds by the shore	*alliteration*	Creates the sound of waves gently and repeatedly hitting the bank
I will arise and go now, and go…		
When the night-air cools on the trout-ringed pools		
And the swish of a skirt		
And the thin anemones		
Only the keeper sees		
The wrinkled sea		
like a thunderbolt		

4 Compare the *structures* of these three poems. You will need to consider:
   • number of stanzas
   • length of the stanzas
   • *rhyme schemes*
   • *rhythm*
   • length of the lines
   • why the poets have chosen that structure.

The Song of the Shirt Thomas Hood

Content and theme

1. What sort of hours does the woman work?
2. What are her clothes and living conditions like?
3. How is her poverty and the work she does damaging her physically?
4. Who does Hood blame for her plight?

Imagery

5. How does Hood emphasise the woman's plight by including the following images in the poem?
   a 'A Shroud as well as a Shirt'
   b 'That Phantom of grisly bone'
   c 'As prisoners work for crime'
   d 'Like the Engine that works by Steam'

Language

6. What is the poet alluding to when he has the woman say she would be better off as a slave in Turkey than as a homeworker in England?
7. How is Hood trying to shame the government of the time by this reference?
8. In line 86 she says that she works 'for Mammon's sake'. Mammon means wealth regarded as an idol or evil influence. What is the effect of this term?
9. How does Hood use references to spring in the eighth and ninth stanzas to make you feel even more sorry for the woman?
10. What other references to nature can you find?
11. In the tenth stanza the woman says that she cannot even cry. Why not? Do you think Hood is exaggerating here? Or does he need to stress this to his readers?

Structure

12. Hood repeats words, lines and stanzas in the poem but sometimes with slight variations. Find these *repetitions* and examine the impact they have in the poem.
13. Why has he chosen a song form for the poem?

Exploring your own response

14. How successful is Hood's poem in making the reader want to do something about home labour?
15. Which techniques used in the poem make you angry about the woman's plight?
16. What aspects of the poem would prevent you from trying to help these women?

This poem is set in the early days of the nineteenth century when people, especially women, did poorly paid work at home. Eventually this domestic work was moved to factories in town.

🔁 **Compare**

Blake's **London** is a 'political' poem, which looks at the situation of the poor and other groups of people. Write a comparison of your responses to **London** and to **The Song of the Shirt**.

The World Christina Rossetti

Content and theme

1. Rossetti comments on the good and bad things in life by comparing night and day. What are the differences in the poem between the world in the day and at night?

2. Which does the poet feel is the truer picture – the world's identity by night or day?

3. What question does she ask at the end of the poem?

Imagery

4. There is a very powerful *personification* of the world as a woman in the poem. Why do you think Rossetti personifies the world as female?

5. Which particular images create an evil, terrifying description of the world?

6. Which day-time images contrast with these?

7. What images of Christian Hell and Greek mythology are found in the poem?

Language

8. How does Rossetti use *alliteration*:
   - to suggest the beauty of day
   - to create the horror of night?

9. In what ways are the following words and phrases effective in the poem:

• Loathsome	• subtle	• void
• leprosy	• satiety	• naked horror

Structure and form

10. Why do you think Rossetti chose the *sonnet* form?

11. How does she reverse our traditional expectations of a sonnet?

12. How does the word 'But' help to structure the first half of the poem?

13. How does the *rhyme scheme* of the poem and the use of indented lines help to get the message across?

14. How does Rossetti build up the sense of horror by the use of punctuation in line 9?

15. Most sonnets change their meaning or content a little after the eighth line. How do the last three lines here differ from the rest of the sonnet?

Exploring your own response

16. Do you agree with Rossetti that the world and our own lives are often more frightening at night?

17. What would you answer to the question she asks at the end of the poem?

 Compare

Explore how the imagery used here compares to that in **The Song of the Shirt**.

In the late 18th and early 19th centuries people were leaving the old agricultural way of life and flocking to cities because of the Industrial Revolution. Several poems written at the time reflect the huge upheaval many people felt.

If you have read the modern novel, *A Kestrel for a Knave* by Barry Hines or seen the Ken Loach film, *Kes*, you will know about the boy who feels more at home in woods and with the ancient art of falconry, than with life in an industrial Yorkshire town and a career down a coal mine.

⇄ Compare

- Which other poems in this section deal with the sense of alienation between town or work and nature?
- Which other poems use images of death when writing about towns?

A Dead Harvest – In Kensington Gardens

Alice Meynell

Many poems in this section deal with the theme that the countryside is superior to the town and that town life is unnatural. This poem fits that pattern.

Content and theme

1 In **A Dead Harvest . . .**, how does Meynell compare town leaves and country leaves?

2 In what ways does the second stanza suggest that the town is inferior and lifeless?

Imagery

3 The poem portrays town life as sterile (unfruitful, unproductive). Meynell says that the rows of hay of the country harvest were 'Raked long ago and far away' as town life takes over.

Compare the sterile images used here to the fruitful images in **To Autumn**.

Language

4 How does the poet use *alliteration* to emphasise the differences between town and country?

Structure

5 How does the *rhyme scheme* of the poem contribute to its effect?

Exploring your own response

6 Choose three poems from the section, which present nature as a life-enhancing force. Explain how the imagery in the poems conveys the poet's feelings to you.

7 Choose two poems from the section which show:
- the peace and beauty of the countryside
- the hustle and bustle of town.

Explore the differences between them.

8 Look at all the four poems in the section set in London. Draw a spider chart with 'London' in the middle. Arrange around it a series of key words which express the poets' attitudes to the city.

How It Looks From Here

This section from **Opening Lines** includes a diverse range of poems. What they have in common is that they are all looking at the world from one person's unique viewpoint.

1 With a partner, read the title of each poem and

- ✓ note down the meanings, ideas, words and images which come into your mind
- ✓ make notes on what you assume the poem will be about
- ✓ quickly read the poems to gain an impression of their content
- ✓ then see if your predictions about the poems were correct.

Use a chart like the one below to make your notes.

Title	What we thought it would be about	What it actually was about
'Defying Gravity'	Science fiction? Something to do with Newton? Defying – going against – disobeying Flying? Not being tied down. Could be gravity in the sense of seriousness. A rebellious poem?	
'Judging Distances'		
'Rat, O Rat...'	A poem about a nasty person?	

2 Now look at the poems where you were able to identify the content more easily from the title and those where you had more difficulty. What does this suggest to you about the nature of that poem and its title?

3 Fit the words below to the poem or poems they most suit in the section:

- fear
- reputation
- dying
- memory
- optimism
- hatred
- happiness
- ageing
- beauty
- reality
- disillusion

4 Choose the poem that, on first reading, made the greatest impression on you. Read it aloud to a partner and talk about how the poem affected you.

In Westminster Abbey there is a Poets Corner, where the nation's most famous poets are buried.

Engineers' Corner Wendy Cope

Wendy Cope uses *irony* in this poem to criticise the nation's attitude to poetry. Irony is when you write the opposite to the truth or to what you really mean. For example, in the line:

> That's why so many poets end up rich

Cope really means the opposite – that poetry is not the way to become a multi-millionaire!

Content and theme

1 Why do you think Wendy Cope was annoyed by the advertisement that the Engineering Council placed in *The Times*?

2 Find examples of her using irony in each stanza.

3 Now you have worked out the ironies, summarise the true picture of:

- a poet's likely lifestyle
- an engineer's lifestyle.

Imagery

4 Cope uses some *cliché* images in the poem. These are usually applied to poets not engineers. Explain how she creates humour in these images:

> - cheerless garrets
> - burn the midnight oil

Language

5 What is the effect of the *rhetorical questions* in line 4?

6 As well as the clichéd images used above, there are some pretty well-worn expressions in the poem. How does Wendy Cope add humour with:

> - Has got it made
> - life is hard
> - It must be hell
> - going down the drain

Extension

Poetry is more important than engineering. Argue the case for and against this point of view.

⇄ Compare

What thematic connections can you find between **Engineers' Corner** and **Judging Distances**?

Structure and form

7 Do you think the *rhythm* and *rhyme scheme* work well and why?

8 How does the *repetition* and the use of *alliteration* in the poem add to the *satirical* effect?

9 Wendy Cope often uses fairly simple, *ballad*-like verse forms and language, which makes her poetry easy to understand. Do you think the form she uses is effective?

Exploring your own response

10 Wendy Cope's poem is intended to make you question the role of poetry and why we read it – or not, as the case may be. What issues has the poem raised for you?

Judging Distances Henry Reed

Content and theme

This poem is about the effect of language, which can describe reality in a poetic and descriptive way or reduce the world to a set of military manoeuvres – like the virtual reality of a computer game.
Reed is learning to use military methods to describe the landscape and what is on it. As you read, imagine the voice of the army trainer and the voice of the recruit who is not paying attention.

1 In the first three stanzas, what has the poet been taught about how to report on a landscape?

2 What is the correct military answer to the question about what the recruit sees in the west? (fifth stanza)

3 Why is his answer only moderately satisfactory?

4 What do you think Reed means, in the last stanza, by saying that the distance between him and the lovers is about one year and a half?

Imagery

The poem uses *imagery* when the recruit gives his own interpretation of the landscape.

5 What are the effects of the images 'shadows bestow/Vestments of purple and gold' and 'like a mirage'?

6 What does the military description leave out which the poetic description includes?

Language

7 What other poetic techniques does the recruit use to describe the scene in the west?

8 What meanings can you find in the term 'dead ground'?

9 What aspects of this military way of describing things are absurd?

10 How does Reed use *colloquial language* to make you laugh?

Structure and form

11 How does the form of the poem makes it dramatic and immediate?

12 How is *repetition* used to create humour in the poem?

13 How does the punctuation suggest someone delivering a lesson?

Exploring your own response

14 Why do you think the poem is called **Judging Distances**? How many meanings can you find in the title?

15 This poem is *satirical* about the military view of the world. Sum up Reed's views on the army, which describes the world in such a way.

Extension

Try to find Henry Reed's poem **Naming of Parts** (it is not in **Opening Lines**). Does it work in a similar way to this poem? How?

Mort aux Chats Peter Porter

and **Rat, O Rat . . .** Christopher Logue

1. Find the real arguments against cats in the poem and those that are for fun.

2. Some of the arguments *parody* racist or sexist arguments (for example, 'There have never been any great artists who were cats' parodies the saying that there have never been any great artists who were women). Find these statements in the poem.

3. How do these arguments add humour?

4. How do they also add an underlying sinister aspect to the poem?

5. How effective is Peter Porter's use of *repetition* and *alliteration*?

6. How does this compare with the way Wendy Cope and Henry Reed use the same techniques?

7. Identify some of the *rhetorical* devices used in the poem.

8. How does **Rat, O Rat . . .** use *irony*? Compare this with Wendy Cope's poem.

9. What makes the poem dramatic?

10. What methods does the poet use to persuade the rat to move next door?

11. Comment on the humour of the following lines:

> * Thank you for noticing my potatoes
> * you could not read it
> * which is forever on our lips

12. What do you find entertaining in this poem?

Comparing poems

13. Compare their:

   * content
   * structure
   * use of *rhetoric*
   * entertainment value
   * methods of creating humour.

14. Both poems parody political speeches. What reasons could you give for not trusting either of the speech-makers in these two poems?

15. Sum up and compare what is comic and serious in the four poems:

   * **Judging Distances**
   * **Mort aux Chats**
   * **Engineers' Corner**
   * **Rat, O Rat . . .**

Mort aux Chats ('Death to cats' for those of us who don't speak French) uses humour as do **Judging Distances** and **Engineers' Corner** .

⊚ Extension

Using the same style as Peter Porter, rewrite the poem from the cat's point of view – and call it: **Mort aux Chiens** !

Defying Gravity Roger McGough

Content and theme

1 'Defying gravity' becomes a *euphemism* for death in the poem. What other meaning could the title have? What examples of the force of gravity does McGough give in the first two stanzas?

2 How do we know that the poet's friend has recently been fit and healthy?

3 What have been the physical effects of his illness? What is the prognosis?

4 How have people reacted to his illness?

5 In what ways will his friend defy gravity in the last stanza of the poem?

Imagery

6 How does McGough use the yo-yo image in the poem?

7 How does he use an *extended metaphor* drawn from rugby in the fifth stanza?

8 In what ways are the living 'weighted down' at the friend's funeral?

9 What different ways are there of interpreting 'Back where the strings are attached'?

10 McGough calls the man's coffin 'a box of left-overs'. How does this help you understand his attitude to his friend's death?

Language

11 Why does McGough call gravity 'one of the oldest tricks in the book'?

12 What is the effect of the following choices of words in the poem?

• abseils	• aw-/Kwardly	• homage
• outwit	• Arranges	

Structure and form

13 How does McGough use the 'book' idea in the first two stanzas?

14 What is the effect of the *enjambment* in lines 12–13?

15 What is the effect of adding speech in the fourth stanza?

16 Why does McGough use brackets in the poem?

17 Look particularly at the *alliteration* and *rhyme* in the last verse of the poem. How do they help to end the poem effectively?

Exploring your own response

18 How does this poem treat death in an up-beat, optimistic way?

19 What do you find moving in the poem?

Sometimes Sheenagh Pugh

Content and theme

1. **Sometimes** is another poem which takes an optimistic slant on life. What sort of fortunate events does Pugh select in the first *stanza*?

2. What area of life is she dealing with in the second stanza?

3. How are events in the last stanza different from what usually happens?

4. How does Pugh end the poem?

Imagery

5. Muscadel is a variety of grape. How does Pugh personify the grape? What is she suggesting by this *personification*?

6. What do you find effective about the image below. What sort of sorrow do you think she means here?

> The sun will sometimes melt a field of sorrow/that seemed hard frozen

Language

7. Why do you think Pugh used *alliteration* in 'faces down frost'?

8. What is the effect of repeating 'Sometimes' and 'some'?

9. What does she mean by 'green thrives' in line 3 and why is 'thrives' a particularly effective word to use?

10. What does 'step back from war' infer about a government's usual approach to war?

Structure

11. Why has the poet changed the *rhyme scheme* in the second stanza?

12. What is the impact of the sound of the *rhymes* 'war/poor' and 'for' in stanza II?

13. What is the effect of the 'to' and 'you' rhyme in the last stanza?

14. There are many run-on lines in the poem which emphasise certain words. Why do you think the poet wanted to stress the words below?

> • faces down • enough • amiss • that seemed

15. Look at the way in which some lines are broken up by *punctuation*. How does this punctuation help to communicate the poet's views?

Compare

What is it about the *tone* of this poem that links it to **Judging Distances**?

Exploring your own response

16. These good things in the poem happen 'sometimes'. If you reverse all the optimism in the poem, what does it suggest about what normally happens in life?

17. Why do you think this would be a good poem to send to someone or to read aloud? Who would you send it to?

A Consumer's Report Peter Porter

A Consumer's Report is based on the format of a consumer questionnaire, in which the customer fills in a long list of questions about a product or their own lifestyle. Peter Porter writes as if he is testing life as if it were a product like a microwave or a new car.

1 The poem takes the form of a *dramatic monologue*. We hear the man's answers but do not know the questions he is being asked. Work out the researcher's questions.

2 Write a summary of the things Porter has found unsatisfactory about 'Life'.

3 Find some riddles in the monologue and say what you think Porter means by them.

4 Explain what makes this a poem rather than a speech or a piece of drama.

5 Find quotations from the poem which raise questions about the nature of life.

I Am a Cameraman Douglas Dunn

6 This poem is about the relationship between art (mostly film in this poem) and real life. Before you read it, write a list of the ways in which a film or television programme is different from reality.

7 Now look at the poem and consider:
- the shortcomings the cameraman sees in his job
- the limitations of film
- why the cameraman's young colleagues think film is the ultimate art form
- why the cameraman disagrees with them
- why real life cannot be captured by film or any other art form, according to the cameraman
- what he means by 'Life disguises itself with professionalism'?
- key words from the poem which portray a rather grim picture of life
- poetic techniques Douglas Dunn uses and the effect they have.

8 Both **A Consumer's Report** and **I Am a Cameraman** try to define the nature of life Summarise the conclusions they come to using a chart like the one below. Do you agree with their depictions of it?

A Consumer's Report	I Am a Cameraman
Life is not very exciting	Life is full of suffering

⇄ Compare

All four poems in this section – **Defying Gravity**, **Sometimes**, **A Consumer's Report** and **I Am a Cameraman** – attempt to make you reflect on life and see things in a new light.

- Look at the methods they use to capture your attention and make you think.
- Which poem does this the most successfully, in your opinion?

In Your Mind Carol Ann Duffy

Content and theme

1 As she goes deeper into the memory Duffy remembers more and more. Look at the first stanza. What do you think makes her want to recapture the memory in the first place?

2 Duffy's main memory in the second stanza is 'A beautiful boy'. What are her main memories in the following stanzas?

3 How do the memories become more intense as the poem progresses?

Imagery

Poets use *imagery* to communicate an idea or feeling to you. You need to think about why they are using that particular comparison. What are the similarities between the two things? What other associations does the image have for you?

4 Analyse the following *similes* and *metaphors* in the poem by completing the following sentences:

a The past is like faded newsprint because . . .
b The moon is like an orange drawn by a child because . . .
c The people's faces are like photographs on the wrong side of her eyes because . . .

Language

5 Now focus your attention on some of the choices of words Duffy has made. Why do you think has she chosen:

- 'muffled' **rather than** 'hidden'
- 'rasp' **rather than** 'noise'
- 'renders' **rather than** 'makes'
- 'Apt' **rather than** 'suitable'
- 'swap' **rather than** 'pay with'
- 'turns up' **rather than** 'intensifies'?

Structure and form

6 Find examples of the following techniques being used to create the impression that memories sometimes flow clearly and at other times are hard to remember:

- questions
- dashes
- one-word sentences
- italics
- *enjambment*
- longer sentences divided by commas.

7 What technique does she use to return, suddenly, into the present in the final line of the poem?

Exploring your own response

8 Which aspects of the poem helped you to imagine Duffy's remembered scene really clearly?

9 What did the poem tell you about the nature of memory? Is this your experience?

Wedding-Wind Philip Larkin

Content and theme

1 To gain an overview of the poem, look at the following aspects:
- what actually happens in the first stanza.
- the woman's feelings at the end of the first stanza.
- the effect of the wind now day has broken in the second stanza.
- the new bride's thoughts and feelings at the end of the poem.

What conclusions can you come to about the couple and where they live?

Imagery

2 In the second stanza Larkin *personifies* the wind, the morning and death. How does this help to suggest the power of the wind?

3 How does he convey the bride's happiness by personifying the morning?

4 How does the personification of death question its power?

5 The bride is clearly full of joy. She compares this feeling to being carried along by the wind – like being swept off your feet. What is meant by the following *similes*?

> - Our kneeling as cattle by all-generous waters
> - like a thread/Carrying beads

Language

6 Larkin uses *alliteration* to create the effect of the wedding-wind for the reader. Where and how does he use alliteration on the letters 'w' and 'l'?

7 His choice of words is effective and thought-provoking. What do you think he wanted to suggest by the following words?

> - Stupid   - borne   - conclude   - ravelled   - perpetual

Structure and form

8 Why does Larkin divide the poem into two stanzas, with the beginning of the second stanza indented.

9 Why does Larkin use *repetition* in the first stanza but not in the second?

10 Why does he use several *rhetorical questions* for the bride's thoughts in the second stanza?

Exploring your own response

11 What is Larkin suggesting about the nature of love, life and happiness by setting a scene of joy in turbulent weather?

12 The details of the couple's identity and the setting is left for the reader to fill in. Why do you think Larkin made these details so vague?

13 What did you find moving about the poem?

Oh Grateful Colours, Bright Looks! Stevie Smith
and The Cat and the Sea R. S. Thomas

1 These two poems use vivid visual description. Use the notes in the chart below to help you look at the description in the poems and compare how the two poems are written.

	Oh Grateful Colours, Bright Looks !	The Cat and the Sea
Content/theme	• Use of words 'grateful' and 'bright' suggest what sort of mood? • Variety of colours – in natural world, in the 'fabricated' world • Point of noticing all these colours is . . . ?	• Simple, basic title • Colours in the first stanza? • Colours suggested in the second stanza? • Is the poem making a particular point?
Images	• Grateful colours – *personification*? Who is grateful exactly? • Fabricated things made beautiful – how? • Image of the puddle made powerful – how?	• Cat's eyes – striking – why? • Similar use of colour to Stevie Smith's? • Setting – how different to Stevie Smith's effect? • Sea's mirror image – mood suggested by 'cold interiors' How similar / different to Smith's puddle image?

Language	• Effect of choice of
	  – coloured (line 9)
	  – vertigo (line 13)
	  – negative (line 14)
	  – Seize (line 15)
	  – colourless (line 18)?
		• Effect of choice of:
		  – matter (line 1)
		  – bare (line 2)
		  – anticipate (line 3)
		  – equation (line 5)
		  – domestic (line 6)?

Structure/Form	• uses *rhyme* • uses *alliteration* • uses *exclamation* • uses *enjambment* • one stanza only	• Brief? • Two stanzas – difference between them? • How does the first stanza relate to the second? • Uses enjambment – how? • 'purr' and 'mirror' – nearly rhyme?

Exploring your own response

2 Now consider the following issues, which connect the two poems.

   a How do they both use colour?

   b In what ways are they almost photographic in their *imagery*?

   c How do the poets give meaning to the images they have chosen? Does one poem do this more than the other?

   d What pictures would you choose to illustrate these two poems? Describe or draw them.

Mirror Sylvia Plath

Content and theme

1 Look at the first stanza and outline the physical characteristics of the mirror. What does the mirror see during the day and night?

2 In the second stanza the content changes to focus on the woman looking into the mirror. Describe the woman's relationship with the mirror.

Imagery

3 Plath uses an *extended personification* in the poem. The mirror is described as a person throughout. Match the aspects of the mirror's character below with quotations from the poem:

- it is accurate in the way it sees people
- it does not judge people before it sees them
- its judgement is fair
- it is honest.

4 In the second stanza, Plath compares the mirror to a lake. The woman searches the 'reaches' of the lake. How does this image help you to understand her relationship with the mirror? How is this image extended to the end of the poem?

5 Why does the mirror call the candles and the moon 'liars'?

6 At the end of the poem, the woman's older face rises 'like a terrible fish'. Why do you think Plath chose this *simile*?

Language

7 Look at the following words in the poem and say what you think they contribute:

• exact • swallow • meditate • faithfully • drowned

8 The language of the poem is quite sinister. Do you agree or disagree? Find words or images from the poem to support your view.

Structure

9 Sum up all the effects of dividing the poem into two stanzas.

10 Most lines in the poem are end-stopped, but some run on to the next line. Look at the lines which run on, especially the final two. What is the effect of this?

Exploring your own response

11 Plath describes the mirror as 'The eye of a little god'. Write down all the ways in which it is god-like.

12 Why do you think this poem is written about a woman, rather than a man?

Bedfellows Don Paterson

Content and theme

1 What does the poem tell you about:
* the wall behind the bed • whose bed it was
* what the present occupier feels and hears?

Imagery

2 The spot behind the bed is called a 'yellow blindspot' and a 'halo'. Brainstorm all the associations these words have for you. One example for each has been done.

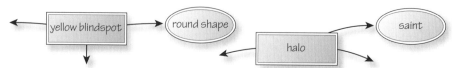

3 What impression of the dead man do you get from the image of his 'greasy head'?

Language

4 The words in this poem are carefully chosen. What do you like about the following:

• hovers	• suffocated
• flowers (why flowery wallpaper?)	• dreary
• rest/my head	• innuendo

Structure

5 The *quatrain* (four-line stanza) structure of the poem is a fairly simple poetic form. What types of poem is it often used for?

6 Why do you think the poet has chosen this stanza form for **Bedfellows**?

7 Why does he run the meaning on from the second stanza to the third?

8 The first and third and second and fourth lines in each stanza either rhyme or nearly rhyme (like 'hovers' and 'flowers', 'rest' and 'wrist'). Why did Paterson choose a *rhyming structure*?

9 What is the effect of the *half-rhymes*?

10 Why are the last two lines in italics?

Exploring your own response

11 There is more than one way in which the men are 'bedfellows'. What is the literal meaning of 'bedfellows' and what is the deeper meaning? What could you quote from the second stanza to help you explain this?

12 Why are the last two lines a 'dreary innuendo'?

13 What is your reaction to this poem? Did you find it funny, sinister and creepy, like a riddle or joke and/or frightening?

Things Fleur Adcock and **The Hare** Selima Hill

Both poems feature a woman waking up in the middle of the night. Before you look at them, discuss with a partner your own experiences of dreams and nightmares, not being able to sleep or waking suddenly.

1   Which woman's experience is more ordinary and perhaps like your own?

2   Which woman's experience is more like a nightmare?

3   Look at the ways in which the way the poems are written. Make a chart with three columns, with the following headings:

• features in both poems
• only features in **Things**
• only features in **The Hare**.

Now write in the following features according to its use in the appropriate column:

• *similes*
• *personification*
• a listing technique
• set in the middle of the night
• *rhyme*
• *antithesis*
• *alliteration*
• repeats words
• one stanza only
• a regular *rhythm*
• long lines.

4   Write a detailed account of how the poets' techniques are suited to the content and theme of their poems. Use your chart and the questions below to help you.

   a   **The Hare** is a mysterious poem. What gives it its mysterious, mythical, fairy-tale quality ?

   b   In what ways is the experience it describes frightening?

   c   What sort of things does the woman in **Things** worry about? How does the poem suggest that they are preying on her mind?

   d   Why does Selima Hill use more *imagery* than Fleur Adcock?

   e   Why does she use rhyme where Fleur Adcock does not?

   f   How does Hill's use of simile bring the woman's experiences to life?

Exploring your own response

5   Many people remember being scared at night when they were a child. What do these two poems tell you about adult fears?

6   Which poem made the greatest impact on you and why?

The 1914–18 War (ii)

OPENING LINES

Some background information on the 1914–18 War is given on page 57 of this book. You do not need to show any knowledge of the history of the war in the examination. The examiners want you to respond to the language of the poems and do not expect or want great chunks of history or biography. Nevertheless, when you are studying the poems, it will help you to know about the conditions of the First World War.

It would also be useful to look at other poems by Wilfred Owen and Siegfried Sassoon, such as those in Section F of **Opening Lines**.

1 Before you read the poems, look at the titles. What groups could you put them into. Copy the circle, then look through the contents page of **Opening Lines** and insert the poem titles into the most appropriate part of the circle.

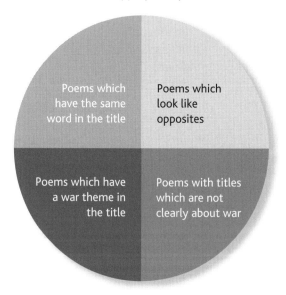

Poems which have the same word in the title

Poems which look like opposites

Poems which have a war theme in the title

Poems with titles which are not clearly about war

2 Now look at the poems. Did your groupings make sense? Did your groupings give you some pairs of poems for which you could explore similarities and differences ?

3 Try organising the poems into some order in terms of war experience. Make a chart like the one below listing the themes and match the poems to the appropriate theme.

Themes	Poems
• joining up	
• going off to war	
• fighting	
• dying	
• grieving	
• remembering the dead	

Joining the Colours Katherine Tynan Hinkson

Content and theme

1 To gain a general feel of the poem, pick out words and phrases that suggest to you:

- that the recruits are young
- that they come from a poor area
- that they are happy to join up
- that they do not really know what they are letting themselves in for
- that they will die.

Imagery

2 There are two main patterns of *imagery* in the poem. List the following images in the appropriate column in a chart like the one below. Explain your choices by considering all the associations of each image, i.e., what ceremonies, colours, feelings do we associate with a wedding day?

- golden
- food for shells
- as to a wedding day
- drab street stares
- Into the dark

Image suggests innocence/naivety	Image suggests their death
'like the lark'	'into the mist'

Language

3 Hinkson uses other words and phrases in the poem, which also add to our mental image of the scene. What do the following suggest about the soldiers?

- all in step
- Smooth-cheeked
- Blithely
- The mothers' sons
- row on row
- careless-gay
- the repetition of High (line 13)

4 Why do you think Hinkson connects the following words through *alliteration*?

- street stares
- glory . . . grave
- gay . . . golden?

5 At the end of the poem she uses many *sibilant* sounds. What is the effect of this?

Structure

6 The poem is written like a *ballad*, but with a short final line in each stanza. Why do you think the poet chose the ballad form here? Why did she choose the short final line for each stanza?

Exploring your own response

7 Look at the final lines of each stanza on their own. What is particularly sad about these lines when read in sequence?

8 What were the poet's feelings about the scene she witnessed?

9 In what ways were your emotions affected by the description?

! Remember

Ballads tell stories and were originally used to spread news. The ballad form is often used for children's verse.

In this poem, the soldiers are not parading through the streets in front of a large crowd, but are quietly going back to the front.

The Send-Off Wilfred Owen

Content and theme

1 This poem is written from the point of view of a fellow soldier. Which part of the poem tells you this?

2 Who has given the soldiers flowers and why?

3 What is the reaction of the few people watching the scene?

4 How many does the poet think are likely to return and to what sort of reception?

Imagery

5 From the beginning, Owen creates a sense of these men being sent secretively to their imminent death. How do these images help to create this effect?

> - close darkening lanes
> - white with wreath
> - Then, unmoved, signals nodded
> - like wrongs hushed-up

Language

6 Owen's choice of words adds to the effect of the *imagery*. What is the effect of the *oxymoron* 'grimly gay' in line 3?

7 The bystanders are described as 'Dull' and 'casual'. What impression does this create?

8 What does Owen mean when he says that he does not know if the soldiers '. . . yet mock what women meant/Who gave them flowers'?

9 Why does he use a *rhetorical question* in stanza seven?

10 How does he use *repetition* in this stanza? What effect does this have?

11 What does the language in the final stanza suggest about the effect war will have on the men?

Structure

12 Owen uses quite an unusual *structure* in the poem. Three-line stanzas are followed by two-line stanzas and the *rhymes* connect the stanzas. He also uses a combination of long and short lines. Look closely at the structure. What kind of mood and feeling does it give to the poem?

⇄ Compare

Compare this poem to **Joining the Colours**, which is also about men going off to die. Look at:

- settings
- verse forms
- standpoint of both poets
- each poet's feelings
- patterns of imagery
- your own response to the poems
- use of contrast.

Recruiting E. A. Mackintosh

and **The Target** Ivor Gurney

Recruiting contains biting criticism of the politicians who sent the soldiers off to war and the journalists who wrote about it. **The Target** is written from the point of view of a soldier who agonises over a man he has killed.

1 Use the notes below to answer the essay question: How do **Recruiting** and **The Target** show that the reality of war is different to the propaganda of recruitment?

	Propaganda	Reality of soldiers' situation
Recruiting	• Soldiers are needed to keep the country safe. • German enemy is comic but also evil ('wicked German foe'). • The sacrifice will be gallant. • War will show their gaiety and strength. **Poet's attitude to civilians** • 'fat, old men' • Cowardly ('Can't you see them … over forty-one?') • 'harlots' • 'blasted journalists' just out for a story	• They will be wounded and/or die ('More poor devils … Waiting to be killed by you?'). • German soldiers just like the British. • The sacrifice will be a martyrdom. • They will be shivering in the 'morning dew'. **Poet's attitude to soldiers** • Honest men • Young ('twenty honest years') • 'Live clean or go out quick'
The Target		• His mother lives in fear of his death. • The man he killed is another mother's son, perhaps her only son. • He needs forgiveness. • God does not seem to care. • War is a 'bloody mess'.

2 Both poems show strong feelings about the war. How do the poets use the following techniques to get their point across in these two poems?

- the four-line verse form (*quatrain*)
- *colloquial* language
- *rhyme*
- *alliteration*.

Exploring your own response

3 Both poems use accessible, straightforward language. What does this suggest about their purpose and the audience they were writing for?

Spring Offensive Wilfred Owen

Content and theme

> Wilfred Owen was a soldier and was killed right at the end of the war. The vivid description in the poem shows us his first-hand experience of battle.

1 Trace what actually happens to the soldiers in the poem by rearranging the following sentences into the right order.

a As they attack they are exposed on an open stretch of ground.
b The soldiers who survive cannot speak of those who died.
c The soldiers have a chance to rest and sleep.
d The enemy opens fire.
e A 'little word' sends them into battle.
f But many soldiers just stare at the place where they will attack.
g Many of the soldiers are shot or blown up.

Imagery

2 The poem is rich in *imagery* of varying kinds. Use a chart like the one below to analyse the following images by type and effect.

- Like an injected drug
- sky burned/with fury
- like a cold gust
- earth set sudden cups/In thousands for their blood
- surf of bullets
- hell's upsurge
- out-fiending

Image	Type of image	Effect of the comparison
'Like an injected drug'	*Simile*	Emphasises the dramatic healing effect of the sun.
'sky burned/With fury'	*Personification*	Suggests the intensity of the bombardment – as if they are being attacked by a vengeful god.

Language

3 It is *ironic* that this devastating, violent offensive should take place in spring. In what way does the poem's title have two meanings?

4 What techniques does Owen use in the second and third stanzas to recreate spring for us? What words does he use to show how spring has affected the soldiers?

5 Which words in the last stanza suggest that the soldiers feel ashamed of the attack and of their survival?

Structure

6 How does the *structure* of the stanzas, especially the use of punctuation and *rhyme*, create a sense of:

- the calm before the storm
- the speed of the attack.
- the survivors' reaction to it

Spring in War-Time Edith Nesbit

Content and theme

Edith Nesbit's poem also contrasts spring and death. Her poem, however, is written from the perspective of one who has been bereaved by war.

1 Nesbit is remembering the lover's lane the couple used to walk along.

   a What is the 'blackthorn snow'?
   b Why do the violets have 'no scent this year'?
   c What does she mean by 'your clay' in the final line?

Imagery

4 Look at the following *images* in the poem. What do they contribute to its theme?

> - sprinkled blackthorn snow
> - Every bird has heart to sing/Of its nest
> - violets
> - red roses

Language

The language is equally easy to understand and Nesbit uses *alliteration* and *repetition* almost in a song-like fashion.

5 What do you think the following lines contribute to the sadness of the poem?

> - **L**ies along the **l**overs' **l**ane
> - **Where** last year **we** used to **go** — **Where we** shall not **go** again.
> - We had heart to **s**ing last **s**pring
> - Will make all the **g**arden **g**ay
> - By **our** wood the violets peer

Structure

6 Nesbit has chosen a *ballad* form for the poem. Why is this an appropriate form for the poem?

7 Which *rhymes* are particularly effective?

8 Why is the final line of the poem shorter than the final lines of the preceding stanzas?

9 What effect does the regularity of the *rhythm* have here?

Exploring your own response

Every aspect of this poem is much less complex than **Spring Offensive**.

10 Explore the following statements. Which comes closest to your own response?

   a It's a bit too simple, with cliché images like 'red roses' for love.
   b The thought of her walking the same route without her lover is really moving.
   c The natural imagery makes the death of the young man seem really unnatural and wrong.
   d Some of the rhymes are too obvious.
   e It deals with a timeless situation that everyone can understand.

Perhaps — Vera Brittain
and **Reported Missing** Anna Gordon Keown

Both these poems were
written by women who had
lost a loved one in the war.
Vera Brittain's is
dedicated to her fiancé
Roland Leighton, whose
death she recounts in her
book *Testament of Youth*.
In Anna Gordon Keown's
poem, the loved one is
reported missing, which
usually meant that they
were presumed to be
dead.

Content and theme

1 As you study the poems, consider:

- whether they were written straight after the death or some time later
- what differences this makes to their content and style.

Imagery

2 Use a chart like the one below to think about the poets' use of *imagery*. What
similarities and differences do you notice?

Imagery	Perhaps –	Reported Missing
nature	'golden meadows'	
time passing		'laughed so lately'
grief		

Language

3 Explore the effect of *alliteration* in both poems, beginning with these examples.
What similarities and differences do you notice?

Perhaps –	Reported Missing
• **s**un will **s**hine	• **l**aughed so **l**ately
• **s**till the **s**kies	• **d**ear and **d**eep–eyed
• blo**ss**oms **s**weet	• **p**iteous **p**latitudes of **p**ain
• **s**ummer wood**s** will **s**himmer	• **s**ummer watercre**ss**

Structure

4 The two poems have similarities and differences in their structure as well. Use these
questions to help you comment on them.

- What is the verse form, *rhythm* and *rhyme scheme* of each poem?
- How is the structure of **Reported Missing** divided in two?

Exploring your own response

5 Explore each of these statements and decide which poem it applies to.

a It is moving because the writer is in denial and will soon have to accept her lover's
death.

b It is moving because the writer has accepted his death and is looking for new hope.

The Seed-Merchant's Son

Agnes Grozier Herbertson

Content and theme

1 The poet chose to make the subject of her poem the son of someone who grows and sells seeds. Why do you think she chose this particular occupation?

2 Which facts about the boy and his life emphasise his youth?

3 How has his father reacted to his death?

Imagery

4 Now look more closely at the *imagery* and the language used to convey the boy's youth and his father's sense of loss. How do the following suggest youth and age?

• child with a child's dreams	• with a child's surprise
• bright eyes	• last glint of his youth is gone
• cheeks all red	• the grey of his head

Language

5 The poet uses *repetition* and *alliteration* in the poem. What effect do the following examples have in the poem?

• His dear, his loved, his only one	• long of limb
• bright, bright eyes	• So still

6 Which words and phrases show the impact of the boy's death on his father? How do they do this?

Structure

7 How does the structure of the poem reflect the themes of youth and age?

8 Why do you think the poet chose a two-line stanza in *rhyming couplets*? Did you find this effective?

Exploring your own response

9 The ending of the poem is mysterious. What do you think the Seed-Merchant meant when he said 'Thank God, thank God!'? Consider some of the following possibilities and choose the one you find the most convincing.

a He is glad that he had a son to sacrifice in the war.

b He is glad that life can still go on by his planting more seeds.

c He is stunned with grief and doesn't really know what he is saying.

d He thanks God that he had a son, even if for a short time.

e He thought that life was over but realises it is not when he looks at the seed.

Do you have another interpretation of his words?

The Parable of the Old Man and the Young Wilfred Owen

Content and theme

Owen's poem also deals with the theme of the contrast between youth and age. Many soldiers in the First World War came to feel that they were being sacrificed by the older generation, who were either commanders safe behind the lines or politicians at home, sending people to die in their thousands.

1 Owen chose to base his poem on the biblical story of Abraham and his son Isaac. In the Bible, when Abraham has demonstrated his obedience, God sends a ram for Abraham to sacrifice rather than his son. The Bible story is meant to emphasise the mercy of God. Abraham is considered the father of the Jewish people and is also important in Islam. The story parallels God's later sacrifice of his own son, Jesus Christ, to redeem the sins of the world.

How has Owen changed the end of the story?

2 Which lines from the poem show that he set the story in the war rather than in the Holy Land?

Imagery

3 Owen has also adapted some of the *imagery* from the Bible story. What is Owen referring to when he says: 'Behold the preparations, fire and iron'?

4 There are some powerful *symbols* in the poem. He calls the ram sent by God, 'the Ram of Pride'. What is Owen suggesting about the government in that it chooses to sacrifice the young men rather than this ram?

5 Why does Owen call the war dead 'half the seed of Europe'?

Language

Owen also uses some biblical language (old-fashioned words like 'clave the wood') in the poem.

6 Find some words which you think are old-fashioned and some which are not.

7 How does the use of both types of language add to the effect of the poem?

8 How does this help Owen use *alliteration* and *repetition* to round the poem off in a powerful and dramatic way?

Structure

The structure supports the impact of the poem.

9 What is the effect of incorporating the speech of Isaac and of the Angel?

10 Why do you think Owen separates the final two lines from the rest?

11 Why do you think he use a *rhyming couplet* at the end? What is the effect of this?

Exploring your own response

12 Why do you think Owen chose this particular parable of Abraham and Isaac to *parody* in his poem?

 Compare

What parallels do you notice between this poem and **The Seed-Merchant's Son**?

The Falling Leaves Margaret Postgate Cole
and In Flanders Fields John McCrae

Content, theme and imagery

1 Both poets use *symbolism*. Brainstorm the symbolism used in both poems to represent the dead. Start by writing down anything you associate with:

Falling leaves

Poppies

The Falling Leaves was written by a woman, Margaret Postgate Cole. In it she uses the leaves to symbolise the fallen soldiers. In In Flanders Fields the speakers are the ghosts of the dead soldiers who have recently been killed.

2 Then look at the following quotations from each poem and decide why you think those symbols were chosen.

The Falling Leaves	In Flanders Fields
brown	Between the crosses
thickly, silently	mark our place
wiping out the noon	We shall not sleep
strewed/Like snowflakes	Flanders fields

Language

3 Both poets use other techniques to convey their feelings about the dead. Find examples of the use of:

• *alliteration*   • *onomatopoeia*   • *repetition*.

What is the effect of each technique?

Structure

4 How does the different structure of each poem suit its content and theme? Use the notes in the chart below to help you plan your answer.

The Falling Leaves	In Flanders Fields
• One long verse – 12 lines	• 3 stanzas of 5 lines, 4 lines, 6 lines
• Rhymes ABCABCDEFDEF	• Rhymes AABBA AABC AABBAC
• Effect of the rhyme?	• Why the short middle verse?
• No full stop until the end.	• Effect of the rhyme?

Exploring your own response

5 What effect do you think the poems were meant to have on readers at the time they were written? What impression did they make on you?

The Deserter Winifred M. Letts

Content and theme

1. Why do you think the poet does not name the soldier?
2. Why did he run and why was this a natural reaction?
3. What punishment was he given?
4. What is the *irony* at the end of the poem?

Imagery

5. Do you think the *imagery* in the poem leads you to sympathise with the deserter? Look at:

   - the *personification* of fear (lines 2 and 17)
   - the comparison to a frightened child.
   - the comparison of the man to a hare
   - the use of the term 'a place apart'

Language

6. Letts chooses her words carefully to put the reader on the side of the deserter. How do the following words and phrases add to your sympathy for the man?

   - Just that
   - The *rhetorical question* – But who can judge him you, or I?
   - 'yearns'
   - wild
   - The **internal** *rhymes* 'throbbing' and 'sobbing'

Structure

7. The poem begins 'There was a man, –' In what ways is the poem structured like a story or fable?

8. The *rhyme scheme* of the poem is interesting in that it repeats the same word at the end of some lines, for example:

   > And so he turned and ran away.
   > Just that – he turned and ran away,

   What is the effect of the *repetitions* and how do they help to structure the poem?

9. How does Letts use *rhyme* to round the poem off dramatically?

Exploring your own response

10. Winifred Letts feels a sense of outrage and injustice at the treatment of the deserter. What are the main ways in which she communicates these feelings?

11. Why do you think the army lied to the families of deserters about the way in which they died? Do you think this was right or wrong?

The Hero Siegfried Sassoon

Content and theme

1. Read the poem and find out what has happened to the soldier. What is his name?
2. How has his mother been informed? How does she react?
3. What has her sons officer told her? What is his real opinion of her son?

Imagery

4. Examine the following *imagery* surrounding the mother. How does this reveal her grief at his death?

> • Something broke
> • quavered
> • lonely woman with white hair

5. Now look at the following imagery used for the son. Why is this imagery so harsh here?

> cold-footed, useless swine

6. Why is the soldier's place of death called 'Wicked Corner'?

Language

7. Sassoon's poem is *satirical*, so you have to think about the implications of the words he has chosen to use. They may mean the opposite to their literal meaning. Look at the following quotations and say what you think he really means:

> • nicely
> • some gallant lies
> • her glorious boy
> • her weak eyes

8. Why do you think he chose the word 'nourish' in line 9?
9. What is effective about the *alliteration* in 'Blown to small bits' in line 17?

Structure

10. The poem takes us through the incident. Trace the story in each stanza.
11. Why does Sassoon use *direct speech* for the mother but not for the officer?
12. How effective is the use of *rhyming couplets* in the poem?

Exploring your own response

13. Is Sassoon on the side of the Brother Officer or is he criticising him?

Sassoon's poem looks at the reality of the war, as does **The Deserter**, but it tells its story in more dramatic form as if we are onlookers at the scene.

The Bohemians Ivor Gurney

and Lamentations Siegfried Sassoon

A 'bohemian' is unconventional, someone who does not conform or 'toe the line'. Both poems are about the effects of war on soldiers – human qualities are taken away, they are not encouraged to be individuals and they are meant to suppress their emotions.

Content and theme

1 In **The Deserter** and **The Hero** we saw that soldiers were not allowed to be afraid, and were despised and punished for this. What kinds of feelings and behaviour are disapproved of in these two poems? Consider these questions to help you.

a What kind of individuality is stamped on in **The Bohemians**?
b How does the speaker in **Lamentations** react to the soldier's grief?

Imagery and language

2 Find quotations from each poem which support the points made below:

The Bohemians	Lamentations
• The poet *satirises* the punishments for not wearing correct uniform.	• The speaker in the poem is insensitive.
• Some soldiers conformed and were promoted.	• He uses a *euphemism* for death.
• Conforming to the army rules was soul-destroying.	• The bereaved soldier is distraught.
• The soldiers no longer need to worry about conforming or not conforming.	• The sergeant cannot understand the depth of his grief.
	• The bereaved soldier hates the war.
	• The speaker sees the grief as almost treasonable.

3 What is the impact of some of the following techniques in each poem:
  • *alliteration*   • use of brackets and dashes   • use of a list ?

Compare

• What similarities are there between **Lamentations** and Sassoon's **The Hero**?

• How does Ivor Gurney's other poem, **The Target** compare to **The Bohemians**? Which did you find more effective, and why?

Structure

4 Use the following list to consider the structure of the poems and how they differ:
  • use of *rhyme*   • breaking up the *rhythm* mid-line
  • use of *iambic pentameter*   • not using a full stop until the end of the poem.

Exploring your own response

5 Both these poems have a conversational, almost throwaway, casual *tone* to them. Why is this deceptive?

6 In what ways does this *ironic* tone have a greater impact than a more straightforward poem?

7 Reading between the lines, what is Sassoon's opinion of the speaker in **Lamentations**? Why do you think he gave the poem that title?

Overview

OPENING LINES

War

Many of the poems in Section C on War dwell on the devastation, destruction and grief caused by war. Some of the poems also suggest that war is often chaotic and that generals are incompetent.

1 To gain an overview of the poems in the section which show an anti-heroic approach to war, complete the following mind-map. You will need to add:
- poems which you think fall into this category
- some colour-coding
- some symbols appropriate to the poems chosen (e.g. fire, a skull, blood stains).

2 What do the poems have in common?

3 Now devise mind-maps for:
- use of *dialogue*
- common patterns of *imagery*
- different settings.

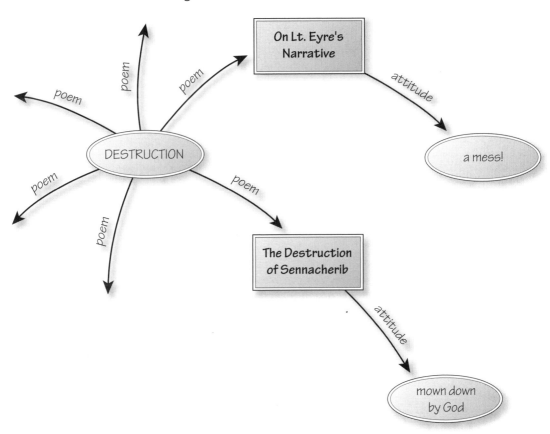

Town and Country

Many of the 'country' poems in this section deal with the theme of time and change. Nature, in Britain especially, lends itself to this theme with the changing cycle of the seasons.

1 To gain an overview of this theme, fill in a chart like the one below. You will need to find quotations from each of the poems which fit the criteria in the left-hand column.

References	The Nymph's Reply ...	To Autumn	Beeny Cliff	The Way Through the Woods	'On Wenlock Edge ...'	Binsey Poplars	The World
To the seasons		'Where are the songs of spring?'					
To the passing of time	'But Time drives flocks from field to fold'						
To change							
To history					'When Uricon the city stood'		
To man changing nature							

2 Now you have a collection of references from this group of poems. Use them to answer one of the following essay questions. They will help you to organise your thoughts on this theme.

a Explore the ways in which **two** poems from the section express the poets' feelings about time and/or change. Remember to refer closely to the language of the poems in your answer.

b The poems in this section concentrate more on the sadness of time passing than on the beauty of nature. Do you agree? Refer to **two** poems in your answer.

c Which **two** poems about the country in this section made the greatest impression on you? Remember to say how the poets made this impression on you by the language they use.

How It Looks From Here

> The poems in Section G are written from various standpoints. Some are inward-looking, some are a critical view on the world, some speculate on the nature of life and death.

1 A useful method of getting to the heart of the poems in the section, and to understand which standpoint they take, is to write a one-sentence summary of each of them. This is also an effective revision exercise. The sentences on each poem have been started for you.

   a   **A Consumer's Report**: The narrator of the poem is someone who has tested . . .

   b   **Oh Grateful Colours, Bright Looks!**: The poet appreciates colour because . . .

   c   **The Cat and the Sea**: The poet connects . . .

   d   **Mort aux Chats**: The poet hates . . .

   e   **Rat, O Rat**: The poet persuades a rat to leave his house by . . .

   f   **In Your Mind**: The poet remembers . . .

   g   **Wedding-Wind**: The narrator of the poem feels . . .

   h   **Judging Distances**: The poet has learned . . .

   I   **Mirror**: The mirror reflects . . .

   j   **Things**: The poet worries . . .

   k   **The Hare**: The poet wakes in the night and . . .

   l   **Bedfellows**: The poet sleeps . . .

   m   **Defying Gravity**: The poet regards his friend's death as . . .

   n   **I Am a Cameraman**: The cameraman feels that life . . .

   o   **Engineers' Corner**: The poet feels that a poet's life . . .

   p   **Sometimes**: The poet hopes that . . .

There is no right answer and you could complete the sentences in a variety of ways. For example, the sentence on **In Your Mind** could be completed as follows:

> - The poet remembers gradually a place she has visited long ago.
> - The poet remembers a foreign place on a wet English day.
> - The poet remembers a place from her past in a series of snapshot images.
> - The poet remembers the sights, sounds, atmosphere of a place in her past.

2 You might find that these summaries limit what you can say about the poem.

   a   Alter the ones you find the least helpful. Analyse why they 'sold the poem short'. In what ways did you have to oversimplify the poem?

   b   Write some summaries of your own about the poems and test them on a friend.

   c   Which poem was the hardest to sum up in a sentence? Why?

   d   Which was the easiest? Why?

The 1914–18 War (ii)

Images of War

> You could group the poems in Section H into those written by men, many of whom took part in the war, and those written by women who lost loved ones.

Many of the poems in this section, written by men, contain strong language and vivid, dramatic and intense images.

1 Look at a selection of these images below and find the poem they come from. Then explain why each image could be described as powerful. Make your analysis in a chart to make comparison easier.

- Fat civilians

- A man might rave, or shout, or sob;
  And God He takes no sort of heed.

- the whole sky burned
  With fury against them

- Blown to small bits

- earth set sudden cups
  In thousands for their blood

- But the old man would not so, but slew his son,
  And half the seed of Europe, one by one.

---

2 Now look at the poems written by women and find quotations from them which fit the images listed in the chart below. Copy the chart and fill in the gaps.

Images	Quotations
Soldiers going to their deaths	
Soldiers as heroes	
Soldiers as children	With his bright, bright eyes and his cheeks all red
Nature	the seed in his hand; There's purple lilac in your little room
Time	
Grief and suffering	

3 Now assess the number of quotations you found in the 'Nature' column. What does this suggest about the standpoint of the women as opposed to the poems written by the men?

4 Attach the following descriptions to the appropriate poem written by one of the female poets. You can use them more than once or not at all:

- lyrical
- elegiac
- realistic
- uses contrast
- angry
- reflective
- resigned
- desperate
- patriotic

Examination preparation

Sample Questions

English Literature, Unit 6: Poetry Pre-1914
Section D: Town and Country

Foundation Tier

1 **Either**

London by William Blake and **Composed Upon Westminster Bridge** by William Wordsworth express very different feelings about the sights and sounds of London. What are these feelings and how do the words of the poets bring these feelings alive for you?

Or

2 What feelings about time and change are expressed in **The Nymph's Reply to the Shepherd** by Sir Walter Ralegh and **On Wenlock Edge** by A. E. Housman? How do the words of the poets make these feelings clear to you?

Or

3 Choose **two** poems from the following list which describe natural scenes in great detail. How do the poets help you to imagine the scenes? Remember to select words and images from the poems in your answer. Choose from:

- **To Autumn** (Keats)
- **The Way Through the Woods** (Kipling)
- **Beeny Cliff** (Hardy)
- **Binsey Poplars** (Hopkins).

Higher Tier

Either

1 Compare the ways in which Wordsworth and Blake express very different feelings about the sights and sounds of London in **Composed Upon Westminster Bridge** and **London**.

Or

2 In **The Nymph's Reply to the Shepherd** and **On Wenlock Edge**, Ralegh and Housman express feelings about time and change. Explore these feelings and the ways in which the poets communicate them to you.

Or

3 Choose **two** poems from the following list which have made the strongest impression on you with their descriptions of natural scenes. Explore the ways in which the poets have created this strong impression through the language they use. Choose from:

- **To Autumn** (Keats)
- **The Way Through the Woods** (Kipling)
- **Beeny Cliff** (Hardy)
- **Binsey Poplars** (Hopkins).

Sample Questions
English Literature, Unit 2: Poetry Post-1914
Section F: The 1914-18 War (i)

Foundation Tier

1 **Either**

How do women react to the war in **War Girls** by Jessie Pope and **In Time of War** by Lesbia Thanet? Remember to refer to the exact words and phrases that the poets use in your answer.

Or

2 In **Of the Great White War** and **Base Details**, Thomas Burke and Siegfried Sassoon write about age and youth in times of war. What feelings do they express and how do their words help you to share these feelings?

Or

3 Choose **two** poems from the following list and write about the ways in which the poets make connections between the war and the world of nature. Choose from:

- **As the Team's Head-Brass** (Thomas)
- **Returning, We Hear the Larks** (Rosenberg)
- **Easter Monday** (Farjeon)
- **There will come soft rains . . .** (Teasdale).

Higher Tier

Either

1 Compare the ways in which the poets present women's feelings about war and their own roles in it.

Or

2 In **Of the Great White War** and **Base Details**, Thomas Burke and Siegfried Sassoon write about age and youth in times of war. Explore the feelings that the poets express and the ways in which they communicate these feelings to you.

Or

3 Choose **two** poems from the following list and explore the ways in which the poets use the world of nature when writing about war. Choose from:

- **As the Team's Head Brass** (Thomas)
- **Returning, We Hear the Larks** (Rosenberg)
- **Easter Monday** (Farjeon)
- **There will come soft rains . . .** (Teasdale).

The style of the exam questions

- All questions require you to be familiar with **two** poems. The questions provide links between the two poems and you are expected to use these links to write about the poems in a comparative way.
- There will always be a choice of **three** poetry questions. One will be extract-based (copies of the poems will be on the paper). You will have **45 minutes** to answer the poetry question which will be worth **25%** of your overall mark for English Literature.
- You will be given guidance on which poems to choose for particular questions.
- The questions always place a strong emphasis on **'language...the words of the poet...the ways...the writing'**, particularly at Higher Tier.

What are the examiners looking for?

1 **Relevance:** you must answer the question they have set and show awareness of the links between the poems noted in the question.

2 **Response:** you must express *your view* of the two poems and take opportunities to point out similarities and differences between them.

3 **Textual Detail:** you must support your views with direct quotation and with detail from the poems.

4 **Evaluation:** you must try to look closely at the way the poems are written – at what makes them *poetry*.

5 **Expression:** you must make sure that you express your ideas clearly and accurately. In English Literature, **5%** of your marks will depend on your accuracy in spelling, punctuation and sentence structure.

The poetry comparison

In this syllabus you have to 'explore relationships and comparisons between texts', which is why *all* the exam questions on poetry require you to look at a linked pair. As you approach a pair of poems avoid:

- writing half your essay on one poem and half on the other without a single cross-reference
- every time you make a point about one poem, making a similar or contrasting point about the other one. This can lead to a list of vague and unimportant points stopping you developing your ideas and getting to the heart of either poem.

The best approach for most candidates is to:

- write an opening paragraph mentioning both poems in relation to the link established by the question, and making some broad comparisons
- look at the first poem in detail
- look at the second poem in detail (with an occasional glance back at the first poem, using expressions such as *'in the same way as'...'unlike'...'in contrast to'...*)
- write a final paragraph, pulling together important similarities and differences from your detailed look at the two poems.

Model answer

> ## Three-point formula
>
> - **Respond** (make a relevant point)
> - **Quote** (support the point with quotation from the text)
> - **Comment** (evaluate the effect of the writing in the quotation).

An answer to the Higher Tier question on **Composed Upon Westminster Bridge** and **London** (see page 131) might use the three-point formula in this way:

> **Response** In contrast to the 'silent...calm' scene which Wordsworth describes, Blake's London is filled with disturbing sounds.
> (focuses on the wording of the question, makes a comparative point)

> **Quotation** Men, infants and chimney-sweepers 'cry', the soldier utters a 'sigh' and the harlot a 'curse'.
> (selects brief, apt quotations...fits them into the sentence neatly)

> **Comment** Blake chooses sounds which suggest misery, fear and anger, and he uses his own sound effects, like the rhyme which links 'cry' and 'sigh' and the strong alliteration which links 'blasts' and 'blights,' to connect these sounds and to make them more distressing.
> (looks directly at the language and at the poet's techniques and the effects of using technical terms appropriately. Makes the connection between the original point and the quotations clear)

Quoting from the text

Notice that all of the direct quotations above are very short, fit neatly into the candidate's sentences and are chosen to make a very specific point. It's much better to use a brief quotation from the text and say a lot about it than to use a long quotation and say very little about it. This is particularly true of poetry where a single word or phrase can pack in so much meaning and effect.

Look at the list of **Dos** and **Don'ts** in the chart below (the examples make use of **Long Distance** in Section E, 'Generations', page 71 of **Opening Lines**):

Do	Don't
• Merge your point and your quotation to avoid repetition. Although Tony Harrison's mother was *'already two years dead'* … **before moving on to make another, more interesting point.**	• Use a redundant quotation repeating the same point – it doesn't add anything. *Tony Harrison's mother has been dead for two years: 'Though my mother was already two years dead.'*
• Refer to e.g. *'the second stanza* or lines *5–8'*. Copying out long quotations wastes valuable time and gets you no extra marks. Better still, just quote the key words or phrases for close attention, e.g. the single word *'raw'* in stanza II reveals a great deal about the father's feelings.	• Use an overlong quotation. *Tony Harrison's father won't accept his wife's death: 'You couldn't just drop in. You had to phone. He'd put you off an hour to give him time to clear away her things and look alone as though his still raw love were such a crime.'*
• Select only the bit you want. *'. . . just the same'* here, belongs to the next line.	• Quote a whole line when you only need part of it. *Tony Harrison faces up to the fact that both of his parents are dead: 'You haven't both gone shopping; just the same.'*
• Mark the line divisions, if your quotation spans two lines of verse. You can do it like this – *'in my new black leather phone book there's your name//and the disconnected number I still call'* – **to avoid starting a new line unnecessarily. Or you can avoid this problem altogether by using shorter, snappier quotations.**	• Ignore line divisions. *Tony Harrison admits that there are some contradictions in his attitude to death: 'in my new black leather phone book there's your name and the disconnected number I still call.'*

Using technical terms

The Glossary on pages 189–192 defines all the technical terms used in this book, but beware of the temptation to approach poetry as if it's a feature-spotting competition. It's easier to pick out technical devices than to analyse their effect, but you will get many more marks for the analysis you do. Examiners want you to write about the **effect** of a particular feature on your understanding and response to a poem, not just to label it. Candidates who notice that the *rhyme scheme* does change at the end of **Long Distance** and then go on to say something about the effect of this (maybe that Harrison changes his view and admits uncertainty about death at the end, and this is reflected in a weaker rhyme pattern) will receive much more credit and higher marks.

Coursework

English

Unit 4: Coursework

You can use any of the post-1914 poets in any section of **Opening Lines** for your English coursework, and any of the pre-1914 poets marked **NC** (i.e. they are on the National Curriculum list). You have a wide choice of poems, and you do not have to write comparatively, but you could use any of the sample Literature exam questions for a coursework task. Several poets appear more than once in this collection so you could extend the range and depth of your essay by looking at two poems by the same poet, for example: Glory and reality in Wilfred Owen's **Disabled** and **The Send-Off**.

Unit 3: Exam instead of coursework

Opening Lines is the set poetry text for the exam alternative to coursework, if your school chooses to follow this route. You will have to study one section, either pre- or post-1914, and there will be a single question on your section.

English Literature

Unit 3 (pre-1914) or Unit 7 (post-1914): Coursework

You could choose to submit coursework based on the poems in **Opening Lines.** Any of the pre-1914 poems are available to you if you are tackling post-1914 poems in the exam (Scheme A) and vice-versa for Scheme B. Any tasks in the style of the sample exam questions on poetry would cover the comparative requirement but you do not have to write comparatively about poetry in your coursework, as long as you cover this somewhere in your folder. If you want to be more adventurous, you could cover two genres at once in interesting combinations, for example: Look at memory and illusions in **Death of a Salesman** (Arthur Miller) and **I Remember, I Remember** (Philip Larkin) (post-1914, Unit 7, Scheme B).

Units 4 and 8: Exam instead of coursework

As with English, **Opening Lines** is a set poetry text for the exam alternative to coursework. There will be a choice of two questions based on the section and the sixteen poems you have chosen.

Combined English/English Literature

Coursework

If you are studying both English and English Literature at GCSE, you might be able to use one piece of coursework for both subjects. So, a single piece of poetry coursework could provide a third of your coursework for both subjects.

OPENING WORLDS

short stories from different cultures

2003–2008

Introduction

The twelve stories in **Opening Worlds** take you into many different cultures and introduce you to a wide range of people, traditions, beliefs and ways of living. The exam questions for both English and English Literature require you to respond to the presentation of different cultures and to make links between the stories.

English

In English, the study of **six** of these stories (for the 'Literary Heritage and Imaginative Writing' exam) will cover one of the main Assessment Objectives – to read literature from other cultures and traditions. The chart below shows which stories can be studied for your examination year.

June 2003 – January 2006		
• Dead Men's Path	• The Train from Rhodesia	• Two Kinds
• Snapshots of a Wedding	• The Gold-Legged Frog	• The Tall Woman and Her Short Husband
June 2006 – January 2008*		
• The Pieces of Silver	• The Young Couple	• Games at Twilight
• The Red Ball	• Leela's Friend	• The Winter Oak

* subject to availability

English Literature

In English Literature, the study of all **twelve** stories (your prose text for exam or coursework) will enable you to cover one of the main Assessment Objectives – to relate texts to their social, cultural and historical contexts and literary traditions.

Context

It is important to be aware of the different cultures and ways of living presented in these stories, but the questions will not be designed to test your knowledge of history or geography. The idea is to get you to look at the way the writer presents the different cultures. You won't get any marks for writing about the effects of the Cultural Revolution in China, for instance, if your ideas are not based on a careful reading of **The Tall Woman and Her Short Husband**.

The short story genre

The sections that follow will help you to explore each story and the short story genre, to link the stories and to prepare for exam questions. In the chart opposite there are some of the key questions and terms. It is easier to write about features like character, plot and setting (**who**, **what** and **where**) than to focus on the writer (and **how** the story is written). Contrast 'Michael Obi is full of his own importance' (**character**) with 'Achebe brings out Obi's self-importance by contrasting it with the calm dignity of the village priest' (**characterisation**). Keeping the writers and their methods in view and looking closely at the writing, rather than just focusing on the story, is often the key to high marks.

Plot

- What are the main events in the story?
- What is the time span?
- Is there a central problem or conflict to be resolved?
- Does the story build to a climax?

Setting

- Where is the story set?
- Does the setting affect the characters or the way the events unfold?
- How does the writer establish atmosphere in describing particular settings?

Character

- Who are the central figures?
- What are their principal qualities?
- Do characters or relationships change in the course of the story?

Characterisation

- How are the characters presented to us? Through direct description? Through the portrayal of their actions, thoughts and feelings? Through their own 'voice' in their dialogue? Through telling the story from their point of view? Through contrast with other characters? Through symbolic detail?
- Does the writer encourage us to take a sympathetic or critical view of the characters?

Theme

- What is the story *really* about – at a deeper level than plot and character?
- Is there a central point, message or lesson to be learned?

Structure

- How is the plot organised?
- Are the events presented in time order?
- Are there time shifts (flashbacks or leaps forward)?
- Are there clear contrasts established?
- Is the ending predictable, unexpected, unresolved?
- Is there a surprise or twist in the tail at the end which helps to illuminate the central themes or answer the questions which the plot has built up?

Point of view

- Is the story told from the point of view of a particular character (John could see that Gwen was upset and he wondered if it was his fault) – we get John's point of view here rather than Gwen's?
- Does the writer use first-person narration (I could see that Gwen . . .) and if so, who is the narrator?
- Does the writer show us everyone's point of view (Gwen was feeling angry with John, and John could see that she was upset)?
- How does the writer's choice of point of view affect our reaction to the story?

Language

- What evidence can you find that story-writers, like poets, make careful language choices to produce particular effects, to set up associations, to create images and moods, and to suggest wider meanings? Your work on images, symbols, metaphors, similes etc. in the poetry section, will be just as helpful in the study of short stories.

The authors' origins and influences

The authors of the twelve stories come from and are influenced by countries (marked on the map below) all around the world:

- Chinua Achebe (Nigeria)
- Bessie Head (Botswanna)
- Nadine Gordimer (South Africa)
- Khamsing Srinawk (Thailand)
- Amy Tan (United States of America)
- Feng Ji-cai (China) Yuri Nagibin (Russia)
- Karl Sealy (Barbados)
- Ismith Khan (Trinidad and Tobago)
- Ruth Prawer Jhabvala (India)
- R.K. Narayan (India)
- Anita Desai (India)
- Yuri Nagibin (Russia)

Mission authorities
(line 4): Many of the
earliest organised schools
in Africa were set up by
Christian 'missionary'
workers from Europe.
Their 'mission' was to
teach young Africans to
read and write, often in
English, and to instil
Christian principles.
Many great African
writers were educated in
Mission Schools. The
teaching of European
Christian values in these
schools was often seen as
an assault on African
traditions and a way for
European countries to
extend their influence.

Dead Men's Path Chinua Achebe

Background

Chinua Achebe was born in Ogidi, Nigeria, in 1930. He has travelled widely throughout his life and has become famous as a novelist, poet, story-writer, broadcaster and teacher, winning many prizes for his writing. His best-known novel, **Things Fall Apart** (1958), has been translated into over fifty languages (and is also an OCR set text for English and English Literature from 2005). Achebe is proud of his African background and identity. He was educated in Christian schools, was the son of a missionary school teacher, and has chosen to write his books in English. He knows a great deal about the effects of European customs and beliefs on traditional African society, and he often writes about this clash of cultures.

What's the story?

1 After your first reading, fix the story in your mind by discussing and agreeing on the main events with a partner. List five more main events in the order they occur, after the first one below.

> 1 Michael Obi is appointed headmaster of Ndume Central School.
> 2 ...

Characters – what are they like?

2 There are three main characters: Michael Obi, Nancy Obi and the village priest. Which of the descriptions in the box below is appropriate for each of the three characters? Make a list for each character, adding some adjectives of your own, and discuss the words, actions and thoughts of each character with a partner. Some of the descriptions below could be applied to more than one character.

- ambitious
- stubborn
- old-fashioned
- self-important
- polite

- patronising
- selfish
- dignified
- petty
- tactless

- respectful
- uncompromising
- superstitious
- dedicated
- image-conscious

The plot – conflicts and twists

3 What differences can you find in the attitudes and beliefs of:

- Michael and Nancy Obi
- Michael Obi and the village priest?

4 Re-read the final paragraph for evidence of final *ironic* twists.

a How is this ending a crushing reversal for Michael Obi and his aims?
b Who do you blame for this outcome?
c Write the 'nasty report' as if you were the Supervisor who inspects the school.

Themes – what is it really about?

Chinua Achebe has said that 'any good story ... should have a message, should have a purpose'.

5 Discuss the following statements with a partner. Which one seems to you to be the story's most central *theme*? Support your conclusion with detail and quotation from the story.

  a Wives have to sacrifice themselves to their husband's career.

  b Progress is often a bad thing.

  c Twenty-six is too young to be a headmaster.

  d It is important to respect the ideas, beliefs and practices – the culture – of other people.

  e Pride comes before a fall.

  f Africa in 1949 was a primitive and violent place.

6 Think about the differences between Michael Obi and the village priest. Make notes about the different ways of life that they represent on a chart like the one below.

Michael Obi	Village Priest
Young	Old
Modern	Traditional

The writer and the writing – Achebe at work

Characterisation

7 You have discussed your responses to the three main characters in question 2. None of these descriptive adjectives actually appears in the text, so how does Achebe present his characters to us and make us respond to them? What is his attitude to the characters he has created? Look at the effects of:

- his direct descriptions, e.g. 'energetic' (line 5), 'frail' (line 35), 'not unhandsome' (line 40)

- the way he refers to his characters at different points in the story, e.g. 'Michael Obi' (line 1), 'Mike' (line 41), 'Obi' (line 5), 'Mr Obi' (line 45), 'the young headmaster' (line 98), 'his young wife' (lines 12–13), 'Nancy' (line 41), 'the village priest' (line 76), 'the old priest' (line 103)

- the point of view he adopts to tell his story and present his characters at different stages, e.g. 'The wives of the other teachers would envy her position' (line 22). Is Achebe telling us this or showing us Nancy's hopes?

- the dialogue he gives to each character, e.g. 'these old and superannuated people in the teaching field who would be better employed as traders in the Onitsha market' (lines 17–19). What is Obi's tone here, do you think? Scornful? Angry? Superior?

A closer look at some language choices

Just as characters like Obi and the priest come to represent, or *symbolise*, different cultures or approaches to life, wider meanings are created by particular language choices.

8 The village priest concludes his argument with the words: 'let the hawk perch and let the eagle perch'. Brainstorm this image. What does it suggest to you? What do you think Achebe is suggesting about the priest's attitudes and beliefs by using this mysterious remark? Is the priest's tone reasonable, calm, helpful, threatening?

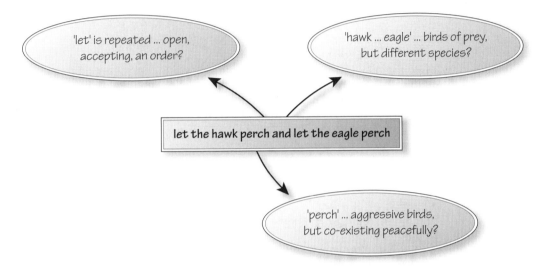

9 Achebe describes Nancy as becoming 'completely infected by his [Obi's] passion for "modern methods"'. Brainstorm the associations of the word 'infected'. What is the effect of this choice of image here?

10 In the same way, recurring features in the story begin to take on wider and more symbolic meanings. What do you think the garden and the footpath come to symbolise as their story develops? Some starting points:

   a Why is the garden important to Obi and Nancy?
   b Why is Obi 'scandalized' (line 52) to see the old woman walk through the marigolds?
   c Why is the garden contrasted with the 'rank neighbourhood bushes' (line 51)?
   d What does the destruction of the garden represent?

Snapshots of a Wedding Bessie Head

Background

'O' levels (line 38):
'Ordinary' level school
exams, which were taken
by sixteen-year-olds
before moving on the 'A'
('Advanced') level. They
have been largely replaced
by GCSEs.

Bessie Head was born in a mental hospital in South Africa in 1937. Her unmarried mother had been placed there by her wealthy white family because Bessie's father was black, and under the racist apartheid laws of the time, their relationship was deemed illegal and shameful. Bessie was placed with a white foster family, who rejected her when they realised that she was a mixed race child. She was raised in a foster home for children, designated as 'coloured', until she was thirteen and then educated in a mission school. She worked as a teacher and a journalist, leaving South Africa after a failed marriage, to take up refugee status in neighbouring Botswana.

Despite the unhappiness in her life and her struggles with mental illness, she managed to produce novels and stories to worldwide acclaim and to become an international example of female endurance and courage. Her writing often tackles race and sex discrimination, the plight of women, poverty, hardship and the painful effects of change in Africa, but is, nevertheless, full of life, joy and feelings of hope. She died in 1986, four years before the release from prison of Nelson Mandela and the removal of apartheid in her native South Africa.

What's the story?

1 After your first reading, discuss and decide on the main story events with a partner. Then add about eight more events in the order they occur in the story to the list below.

> **1** Kegoletile's relatives arrive with an ox for the wedding feast.
> **2** Neo completes her 'O' level exams.
> **3** . . .

2 Now put your list into chronological (time) order. You will have noticed that the writer does not tell the story in strict chronological order (e.g. event number 2 above happens a long time before event number 1).

3 What do you think Head gains by starting the story with the wedding preparations and then going back in time to fill in details of the story before returning to the wedding at the end?

4 How much time does the whole story cover – including the flashbacks? (Note: Neo is six months pregnant, with her second child, at the time of the wedding).

Characters – what are they like?

5 There are three main characters: Neo, Kegoletile and Mathata. Look through the story at all the references to these characters and underline all the descriptions, speeches, actions in the story which support or contradict the statements about the characters opposite:

a Neo's education has made her arrogant and unpopular.

b Neo has a condescending manner.

c Neo does not feel threatened by Mathata's pregnancy.

d Neo is not as confident as she appears.

e Kegoletile is generous.

f Kegoletile has a pleasing manner and is very popular.

g Kegoletile's heart tells him to marry Mathata.

h Kegoletile allows himself to be pressured into marrying for money.

i Mathata is a contrast to Neo in many ways.

j Mathata is easy-going, cheerful and content with her life.

The plot ... conflicts and twists

6 What evidence of conflict can you find in the following?

a Neo's relationship with her family and her society. Why exactly is she so unpopular? Which moment in the story represents a turning-point for Neo?

b Kegoletile's feelings about choosing a wife. Read in particular the paragraph beginning at line 82.

7 One of the central narrative questions that keeps us reading is 'Who will Kegoletile marry?' Do you think that he makes the right choice?

Themes —what is it really about?

8 The story gives us 'snapshots' of a particular society. Consider the following statements about this society. Find evidence from the story to show how far you agree or disagree with each statement.

a It's acceptable for men to sleep around.

b Women are subservient to men and are not possessive.

c Men and women have very different roles and responsibilities.

d Children are important to a marriage.

e It's important to show respect to your elders.

f It's important to maintain traditions.

9 The story ends with Neo's aunt pounding the ground and urging her to 'Be a good wife!' What do you think it means to 'be a good wife' in this society?

10 The society, like many others depicted in **Opening Worlds**, is changing. At the start, one character announces: 'This is going to be a modern wedding' (line 23). What signs can you see that:

• education and making money are becoming more important than working on the land

• Neo is an unusual young woman in this society

• Neo and Kegoletile may break with tradition in their married life?

The writer and the writing – Head at work

Characterisation

11 What is Head's attitude to the characters she has created? How does her writing affect the response of the reader to these characters?

NEO. Neo is described as 'an impossible girl with haughty, arrogant ways' (lines 36–7). Is this Head's point of view or the view of Neo's relatives? Neo is described as 'the silly girl' (line 111). Is this the writer's view or the aunt's?

MATHATA + KEGOLETILE. Re-read the important paragraph beginning at line 82 and the descriptions of Mathata and Kegoletile there. Can you find evidence that the author:

- approves of Mathata and Kegoletile, emphasising their charm
- feels sympathy for Kegoletile's 'conflict'
- disapproves of Neo?

Can you find evidence that Head:

- feels sympathy for Neo as a woman wronged by a faithless fiancé
- feels that Kegoletile uses and has no respect for women
- sees Mathata as a doormat and a brainless bimbo?

Arrange your analysis as a chart if it helps you to compare the treatment of Neo as opposed to that of Mathata and Kegoletile.

A closer look at some language choices

Setting

12 The title **Snapshots of a Wedding** suggests a series of photographs. Look closely at the language in the first paragraph. How is the writer creating images to establish a 'haunting, magical' atmosphere for the morning of the wedding? Pick out words and phrases which create this dream-like and expectant atmosphere. Look out for and comment on the effect of:

- water *imagery, metaphor, simile*
- descriptions of the dawn light and its effect
- descriptions of unusual sounds.

Symbolism

13 We are told (line 96) that Kegoletile stares at 'an empty space beside him'. What is Head suggesting about Kegoletile's feelings in this *symbolic* gesture, do you think?

14 What is the symbolic significance of some of the rituals like:

- the request for water (line 141)
- the chopping at the ground with the hoe (line 158)
- the dance (lines 169–70)?

The Train from Rhodesia Nadine Gordimer

Background

Nadine Gordimer was born in South Africa in 1923 to an English-speaking family. Her father was a jeweller from Latvia of Jewish descent and her mother was British. She wrote her first published story at the age of fourteen. Despite her wealthy background and comfortable life in the 'white' areas of Springs, Transvaal, near Johannesburg, she became an outspoken critic of the racist apartheid regime with its strict segregation of people according to their colour. She was also critical of the ways in which the white European minority controlled the black African majority and exploited the rich natural resources of the land they had colonised. Much of her writing is concerned with this and her books were often banned in her native land. She is one of the most admired modern writers for her novels and her short stories, and she was awarded the Nobel Prize for Literature in 1991, becoming only the eighth woman to win the prize in its ninety-year history.

> **Rhodesia** (Title): The name of a former British colony in South-East Africa, neighbouring on South Africa. Achieved black majority rule and independence in 1980 and was renamed Zimbabwe.
>
> **piccanins** (line 10): Black African children.
>
> **vandyke** (line 36): Anthony van Dyck was a famous 17th-century Flemish painter. He painted many British aristocrats, who had short pointed beards – fashionable at the time and now known as 'Vandykes'.
>
> **Three-and-six** (line 81): Three shillings and six pence. In the pre-decimal British currency there were 20 shillings in a pound and 12 pence in a shilling. 'Three-and-six' might have been a fair price for the carving in the 1950s.
>
> **baas** (line 82): South African word for 'Boss', used to address overseers, Europeans and white people generally.

What's the story?

1 This is a descriptive and subtle story. On the surface very little actually happens, but there is a story-line and some of the key events may become more significant as you re-read the story. Put the following events into chronological order:

a The train arrives at the little station.

b The young married couple buy lots of souvenirs on holiday in Rhodesia.

c The stationmaster's children collect two loaves of bread.

d The old man runs after the train to sell the lion for less than half the asking price.

e The young woman rejects the lion angrily as the train leaves the station.

f The young woman asks the old man to show her the carved lion.

g The young man throws one-and-six from the train.

h The girl throws chocolates from the train.

Characters – what are they like?

2 The characters, like the story-line, seem undeveloped. The three central characters are the young married couple and the old vendor but Gordimer does not give them names, does not give them much dialogue, and appears to avoid direct description of what they are like. Feelings are revealed in a more indirect way. Look at the following quotations. Describe the context for each and decide what they might reveal about the characters' feelings at that point in the story.

a The old man held it up to her still smiling, not from the heart, but at the customer. (lines 35–6)

b The young man swung in from the corridor, breathless. He was shaking his head with laughter and triumph. Here! he said. And waggled the lion at her. One-and-six! (lines 134–6)

c To give one-and-six for that. The heat of shame mounted through her legs and body and sounded in her ears like the sound of sand pouring. (lines 171–3)

The plot – conflicts and twists

3 Look for evidence of the contrasts between:
- the worlds inside and outside the train
- the attitudes and feelings of the young man and the young woman.

4 If there is a twist at the end of this story, it is the young woman's rejection of the lion carving which her husband has bought for her and which she obviously admires. The central narrative question is: **Why does the young woman reject the carving?**

Themes – what is it really about?

5 An *allegory* is a story in which the details have a wider, *symbolic* significance throughout. Could this story be seen as an allegory, showing the sad story of a racially divided South Africa? Pick out details from the story which might support the following statements.

a White people and black people live separate lives.

b White people enjoy privilege and black people endure poverty.

c White people have power over black people and force a humiliating dependency on them.

d White people exploit the labour and creativity of black people.

e Some white people feel guilty about the exploitation of black Africans and of their beautiful country.

f White Europeans arrive, use South Africa for their own ends and move on; they are never really part of the country.

The writer and the writing – Gordimer at work

Characterisation

6 Gordimer describes the people and the setting in the third-person (he, she, they) but does show us the young woman's *point of view* on several occasions. For instance in line 93 we are told, 'Her eye followed', so we are seeing what she is seeing. Find the sections of the story where Gordimer is using the young woman's point of view.

7 What do you learn about the young woman and her feelings (about her holiday, about the lion, about her husband, about her life) from these sections?

8 What is the effect of telling the story in this way? Do you feel closer to her than to the other characters in the story?

A closer look at some language choices

Setting

9 In the first twenty-six lines, Gordimer could be said to be setting the scene, but she is doing much more than providing background or describing a pretty sunset. As you saw in question 5, the story might be seen as an *allegory* showing racial divisions, but descriptive detail can also have *symbolic* significance beyond its surface meaning. Think about the following features of the opening description and answer the questions.

   a How does Gordimer suggest the poverty of the people at the station?

   b How does she contrast the train with the station?

   c Why does she *personify* the train (it 'called out', it has a 'body', it is 'gasping') here and throughout the story?

   d Why is there 'no answer' when the train 'called out' at the beginning and at the end of the story?

   e Why does she describe barriers between people ('The stationmaster's wife sat behind the mesh of her veranda') here and throughout the story?

Symbolism

10 Look closely at the descriptions of the lion (lines 33–41, 141–3 and 168–71) and answer the questions.

   a What do you usually associate with lions? What do they represent for you?

   b What impressions of the carving does the writing give you here?

   c Does the writing convince you that the carving is a 'beautiful piece of work' (line 160)?

   d The carving ends up 'on its side in the corner' of the train compartment. What does this suggest to you and how does it make you feel?

The Gold-Legged Frog Khamsing Srinawk

Background

Khamsing Srinawk was born in Thailand in 1930. His family were buffalo farmers, but supported his school education so that he was able to study both economics and journalism at university. He has become one of Thailand's best-known modern authors and is often described as 'the master of the Thai short story'. His stories are often concerned with the kind of life he knew as a child and he writes with great sympathy about the struggles of the Thai villagers in tending their rice crops and trying to live off the land. However, the pen-pushing and unfeeling authorities, who control the hard-working peasant farmers, are often the target for his *satire*. This story is translated from its original Thai version.

What's the story?

1 A great deal happens in a short time in this story. After your first reading, complete this list of the ten main events in the story to make clear what happens:

> **1** Nak rests exhausted against a tree as he travels home to his village.
> **2** He sees a whirlwind and suffers from sunstroke.
> **3** Nak and two of his small children hunt for frogs.
> **4** ...

2 Now put your list in *chronological* order. You will have noticed that event number 3 takes place before event number 2.

3 What period of time does the whole story cover?

4 How is the *structure* of this story similar to **Snapshots of a Wedding**?

5 What does Srinawk gain from telling the story of the snake-bite and the trip to the District Office, as if Nak is remembering it as he makes his way home?

Characters – what are they like?

6 The character of Nak dominates this story. Think about the following statements about him. Can you support them with references to the story? Do you agree with all of them?

a He works hard to provide for his family.
b He is a devoted father.
c He blames himself for what happens to his son.
d He does all he can for his dying son.
e He is obedient, respectful, law-abiding and easily swayed.
f He has a sense of humour despite everything.
g He cares more about money than about his son.

7 Compared with Nak, the other adults in the story appear highly unsympathetic. Select details from the story which you feel demonstrate the unpleasantness of:

- the deputy district officer
- other villagers.

The plot – conflicts and twists

The reader is faced with two central *narrative* questions, which drive the story and build suspense: Will Nak's son survive? Will Nak get the 'many children money'?

8 Nak is faced with an agonising decision and is tormented by conflicting feelings.

a What is the exact nature of the decision Nak has to make?

b Do you feel that he makes the right decision?

9 Re-read the final section (from line 130 to the end), describing Nak's return to the village and the sad 'twist in the tail'.

a How are Nak's hopes raised and then cruelly dashed in this section?

b What do you think the villager means in the final sentence (lines 141–2)? (Remember the government rule about which families can claim the 'many children money'.)

c Explain the grim *irony* in the idea of Nak being 'lucky'.

Themes – what is it really about?

10 Nak thinks to himself (lines 103–4) 'All you do is suffer if you're born a rice farmer and a subject.' Consider the following and for each point give evidence from the story of the ways in which Srinawk builds up the feeling that Nak is born to suffer and that the life of a rice farmer is anything but 'lucky'.

- his extreme poverty
- his physical suffering
- his emotional suffering
- the harsh climate and infertile land
- he is bossed around and cruelly treated
- fate is stacked against him.

The writer and the writing – Srinawk at work

Characterisation

11 Srinawk tells the story in the third person but gives us Nak's point of view – what he is seeing, remembering, thinking or feeling. Look at this example of Srinawk writing from Nak's *point of view*. What effect does this approach have on your feelings for Nak?

> Vague anger again spilled over as his thoughts returned to that moment. If only he had gone home then, the poor child would be all right now. It was really the last crack. (lines 37–40)

12 Srinawk's writing produces rather different feelings about the character of the deputy district officer. He doesn't attack him directly but he makes use of some heavy *irony*. Why you think Srinawk:

- gives him a 'fat face' (line 96)
- has him describe his 'scribbling' (line 102) as 'working' (line 98)
- gives him a long lunch break
- points out that he 'had the kindness to say a few words' (line 109)?

A closer look at some language choices – building tension

13 How does Srinawk catch the attention of the reader and build suspense up to the dramatic moment of the snake bite (the first 45 lines)?

14 What do you think is the effect of the following techniques (we have already touched on the first two in question 5 and 11 above):

- using the point of view of Nak, the father
- telling the story as if Nak is remembering it on his way home
- using **The Gold-Legged Frog** as the title
- *personifying* the sun as 'determined to burn every living thing' (line 1)
- using *symbolic* detail like the falling leaves (lines 2–4 and repeated lines 130–1)
- describing the effect of the whirlwind and the beliefs surrounding it (lines 7–10 and mentioned again in line 132)
- posing questions and delaying the answers – why is Nak 'exhausted' (line 4), 'afraid' (line 10) and 'anxious to get home' (line 10) and why is he thinking of his 'little son' (line 19)?
- hinting at the crisis before revealing it – 'If only he had gone home then, the poor child would be all right now' (lines 38–9).

Two Kinds Amy Tan

Background

Amy Tan was born in Oakland, California, in 1952. Both her parents were Chinese immigrants who escaped to the USA from the turmoil of Chinese civil war in the 1940s. By the time Tan had finished high school she was in constant conflict with her mother, reacting against the strict musical training that was forced upon her and choosing to follow her boyfriend to college and to study English rather than medicine. Mother and daughter did not speak for six months. Tan worked with children with disabilities and then as a business writer before turning to fiction and studying jazz piano. She visited China for the first time in 1987, taking her mother and reuniting her with the daughter from a previous marriage whom she had been forced to leave behind nearly forty years before. The trip gave Tan a new understanding of her Asian-American background, of her mother and of their troubled relationship, and she completed a series of autobiographical short stories. Her first novel, **The Joy Luck Club** (1989), was a huge success and has been translated into more than twenty languages, including Chinese.

1949 (line 10): after three years of Civil War and suffering, Mao Tse-tung led his Communist forces to victory and established the People's Republic of China in 1949.

Shirley Temple (line 15): Shirley Temple was a cute, curly-haired child star of Hollywood movies in the 1930s.

Formica (line 50): cheap plastic coating.

Chinatown (line 65): the area of the town which has a mainly Chinese population.

The Ed Sullivan Show (line 100–1): a record-breaking American TV show, which was a fixture on Sunday evenings from 1948 to1971, and was famous for the variety of its musical, comedy and novelty acts.

What's the story?

1. This is one of the longest stories in **Opening Worlds** and it covers the longest time span (well over thirty years) in three main sections. List the main events for each section:

> 1 Before Jing-mei is born – the events leading up to 1949.
> 2 (Biggest section) The year of 'training' when Jing-mei is nine.
> • Jing-mei's mother takes her to a beauty school
> • Jing-mei's mother begins testing her
> • (six main events should be enough in this section)
> 3 Later life – when Jing-mei is in her thirties.

2. Which two moments would you pick out from your lists as the most important in the story? Why?

Characters – what are they like?

3 There could be a range of reactions to Jing-mei and her mother – the two main characters. Can you justify the following statements by quoting particular descriptions, speeches or actions from the story?

> **Jing-mei's mother:**
>
> - works tirelessly and unselfishly to provide opportunities for her daughter
> - bullies her daughter and refuses to listen to her
> - pushes her daughter to achieve for her own selfish reasons and not for her daughter's sake.
>
> **Jing-mei:**
>
> - does her best to please her mother
> - is lazy and ungrateful
> - is unforgivably rude and cruel in the way she speaks to her mother.

The plot – conflicts and twists

4 The mother–daughter conflict is at the heart of the story. Think about the reasons for the conflict and the way it develops in the following extracts:

a America was where all my mother's hopes lay. (line 9)

b And after seeing my mother's disappointed face once again, something inside of me began to die. (lines 77–8)

c I won't let her change me, I promised myself. I won't be what I'm not. (lines 88–9)

d Three days after watching *The Ed Sullivan Show*, my mother told me what my schedule would be for piano lessons and piano practice. (lines 135–6)

e And then I decided. I didn't have to do what my mother said anymore. I wasn't her slave. This wasn't China. (lines 311–12)

f 'Only two kinds of daughters,' she shouted in Chinese. 'Those who are obedient and those who follow their own mind! Only one kind of daughter can live in this house. Obedient daughter!' (lines 332–4)

5 The plot also throws up some twists:

- a *comic irony*. Why is Mr Chong the only one to enjoy Jing-mei's performance in the talent show (lines 265–6)?

- the final ironies:

  a What is Jing-mei's reaction to the gift of the piano (lines 368 and 378)?
  b Why does she take the Chinese dresses home (lines 387–90)?
  c What does she realise in the final paragraph and why is the timing sad?

Themes – what is it really about?

6 Which of the following ideas seems to you to be most central to the story?

    a You will get nowhere without discipline and effort.

    b Parents cannot live their lives through their children.

    c America is competitive, but also a land of freedom and opportunity.

    d Parents have to learn to let their children live their own lives.

    e Good parenting is not putting your children under pressure.

7 How does the title relate to the story's central themes? Does the story suggest that:

    • the mother and daughter have two different kinds of personality?
    the mother and daughter are caught between two different kinds of cultures – Chinese and American?

    • there are two different kinds of daughters – the obedient and the wilful?

    • there are two different kinds of children – the remarkable and the ordinary?

    • there are two kinds of approaches to life – the easy way and the hard way – and they should be kept in balance? (Chinese philosophy stresses the importance of keeping opposing forces, yin and yang, in balance).

The writer and the writing – Tan at work

Characterisation and the narrator

This is the only story in the collection which uses a character as a first-person *narrator*. Tan uses Jing-mei as the 'I' who tells the story – an approach which is particularly popular among American writers. Think about the following questions to help you to explore the effect of this approach.

8 When exactly is Jing-mei writing the story and why is this important? She describes life as a nine-year-old, but she is not writing at that time.

9 Are you more sympathetic to Jing-mei because it feels as if she is sharing her feelings with you first-hand? Look at lines 76–89, for instance?

Characterisation and dialogue

10 Look at the difference between Jing-mei's dialogue and her mother's dialogue. Why does Tan create this difference, do you think?

11 Why does Jing-mei's mother revert to Chinese at certain times, e.g. line 332?

A closer look at some language choices

The language of comedy

12 Pick out and explore out some moments where you think Tan gives us the humorous point of view, logic or language of a nine-year-old girl. The description of the Chongs (lines 152–62) is one example.

The language of conflict

13 Pick out and explore the effect of the verbs which Tan uses to convey the actions of Jing-mei's mother, especially in her dealings with her daughter. Line 324 will give you three to start with.

The Tall Woman and Her Short Husband Feng Ji-cai

Background

Feng Ji-cai was born in Tianjin, China, in 1942. He studied painting as a young man and became very interested in traditional Chinese arts and customs, combining teaching with writing and study. It is as a novelist and short-story writer that he has won international fame and he is now one of China's best-known writers. He lived through the period of China's Cultural Revolution (1966–76) when the Chinese leader, Chairman Mao Tse-tung, attempted to create a new Communist society. Mao wanted to break with the past, create equality and encourage community effort, especially hard physical labour. In practice, this meant that individuality became the subject of envy and suspicion and 'intellectuals' (writers, artists, teachers) and professional people (doctors, lawyers, managers) were often persecuted. Over 100 million people were persecuted during this decade and half a million were killed or committed suicide. Many schools, museums and libraries were closed. Feng Ji-cai later collected and published a series of eye-witness testimonies about these tragic events, entitled *Ten Years of Madness*. **The Tall Woman and Her Short Husband** is translated from its original Chinese version.

> **measurements** (lines 19–21): She is 5ft 8ins; he is 5 ft 1 in, approx.
>
> **yuan** (line 118): Chinese unit of currency. 180 yuan is about £16 today.
>
> **foreign capitalists** (line 138): most European countries and the United States were viewed with suspicion by communist countries like China at this time because their economic systems were based on capitalism – the private, rather than communal, ownership of capital and property.
>
> **Deng Tuo** (line 221): a poet and historian who was seen as an opponent of the Cultural Revolution. He was a co-writer of a magazine column called *Notes from the Three Family Village* (see line 223).

What's the story?

1 This story covers more events, both personal and political, and a longer period of time than many of the stories, so it is very important to sort out the details and the time span. Complete the list of the most important things that happen to Mrs Tall.

> **1** She moves into Unity Mansions with her husband
> **2** She is mocked by old ladies and children
> **3** . . .

2 Then decide on a similar list for Mr Small. Many items will be the same.

3 How much time does the whole story cover, approximately? When is the story set?

Characters – what are they like?

4 There are three main characters: the married couple and the tailor's wife. Which of the descriptions below fits the married couple and which applies to the tailor's wife? Support your views with evidence from the story of these qualities.

- hard-working
- prying
- dignified
- gossipy
- malicious
- courageous
- self-important
- unconventional
- envious
- cynical
- self-contained
- reserved
- loving
- loyal
- uneducated

The plot – conflicts and twists

5 Re-read the parts of the story that deal with the rumours spread about the married couple and the charge made against them. Then decide on your responses to the following questions.

a What is the truth about this couple and their relationship?

b Why are they subjected to so much gossip and persecution? (In lines 206–7, for instance, we are told that Mrs Tall had 'seen through' the tailor's wife. What do you think she has realised about the motives of her chief tormentor?)

6 How is the decline of Mr Short and Mrs Tall mirrored by the rising fortunes of the tailor's wife? Why is this so *ironic* and unfair? Pinpoint exactly where this key plot reversal takes place in the story.

Themes – what is it really about?

7 Feng's stories often take the form of *fables* – stories which teach moral lessons. Decide on the important lessons which could be drawn from this story. The opening section on the subject of trees should give you some ideas.

> ▶ **Starting points**
>
> - You should learn to accept and respect differences and individuality.
> - You shouldn't judge by appearances.
> - It's a mistake to stand out from the crowd.
> - Everybody needs good neighbours.
> - Beauty is in the eye of the beholder.

Now add your own list of lessons.

8 Feng describes the events of the Cultural Revolution as a 'disaster' (line 130) and 'that period of lunacy' (line 138). He also describes what happens in Unity Mansions as a 'microcosm' (line 131) – a small-scale version – of what was happening in China generally at this time. Re-read the description of the 'struggle meeting' (lines 149–229).

a What do you feel about the events described here? Are they unfair, ridiculous, frightening, moving, laughable...?

b How does Feng make his own feelings about the meeting (and the Cultural Revolution) clear to us in this section? What is ironic about the name 'Unity Mansions', for instance?

The writer and the writing – Feng at work

Characterisation

9 Feng gives his central married couple no *dialogue* and seldom shows us their thoughts or describes their characters directly. He doesn't even give us their names. Nevertheless he manages to produce a strong impression of their strengths and of their love for each other by the end of the story. Look at the following quotations.

a Questions and denunciations were fired at her, hysterical screams, angry shouts and threatening growls. But she simply shook her head gravely and sincerely. **(lines 182–4)**

b The next morning when Mrs Tall led her son out, her eyes were red. No one would speak to her, but they all saw her red, swollen eyes. Those who had denounced her the previous day had a strange feeling of guilt. **(lines 247–50)**

c Every morning and every evening Mr Short helped her twice round the yard, painfully and slowly. By hunching up his shoulders he was able to grip her crooked arm in both hands. It was hard for him, but he smiled to encourage her . . . This was a pathetic yet impressive sight, and the neighbours were touched by it. Now when they met the couple they nodded cordially to them. **(lines 297–304)**

d She sat in the gatehouse sizing up its furnishing as she proposed this match to rich Mr Short. Smiling all over her face she held forth with gusto until suddenly she realised that he had not said a word, his face was black, and behind him hung a picture of him and Mrs Tall on their wedding day. **(lines 321–5)**

e The final paragraph. **(lines 327–34)**

How does Feng present these characters to us here and make us respond to their strength of character and love for each other? Think about:

- the way he reveals their feelings through their physical appearance
- the way he contrasts them with other characters (especially the tailor's wife)
- the way he presents the changes in the neighbours' response to them.

A closer look at some language choices – 'Hooking' the reader

10 At the start of the story, Feng uses several techniques to capture the reader's attention. In a way, he puts the reader in the position of a nosey neighbour. Re-read the first 61 lines and give examples from the text of the following techniques:

- addressing the readers as the second-person (as 'you')
- asking questions
- telling the reader what to do and what to think
- using *colloquial* (chatty) language generally
- showing us the central couple from the point of view of the nosey neighbours
- suggesting that there are unanswered questions about the couple
- describing them in humorous terms (especially using some unusual *similes*).

The Pieces of Silver Karl Sealy

Background

Karl Sealy was born in 1922 on the Caribbean island of Barbados, the son of an engine-fitter and one of eight children. He excelled at school and went on to train to be a teacher and spent his career teaching in the secondary schools of Barbados. He married in 1962 and had two sons. He published a number of stories and poems in the *Trinidad Guardian* and became a storywriter and a poet with an international reputation. He was also an outstanding chess player, who represented his country at the highest level of competition. He died in September 1993. Like other Caribbean islands, Barbados was run as a British colony for centuries and only achieved full independence in 1966, so that the British influence – on education, language and in many other spheres – is very strong.

What's the story?

1. The action of this story covers twenty-four hours in the life of Clement Dovecot, from one morning at school to the next. What is he most likely to remember about the events of this day? Compete the following list with eight more main events.

> 1. He is left standing in assembly because he has not contributed to the Headmaster's leaving present.
> 2. The acting Headmaster, Mr Chase, makes him stand on the platform.
> 3. . . .

Characters – what are they like?

2. Clement is treated very differently by Mr Chase and by his sister, Evelina. Place the quotations on this and the next page in the context of the story and then decide what they show about Mr Chase, Evelina and the differences between them.

Chase
• stout, pompous
• The smaller boys straightened and stiffened under his cold gaze
• emitting an untrue, faltering note
• showed the gleaming gold of his teeth
• fierce-eyed and unsmiling
• under the threat of the lash
• spent some minutes more making the hapless boys the laughing-stock of their schoolfriends
• Mr Chase eyed their bowed heads in enjoyment

Brutus' ingratitude...

(lines 89–92): Mr Chase is misquoting from Shakespeare's *Julius Caesar*. Caesar was assassinated by a group of men, including his friend, Brutus.

Mark Antony, a loyal friend, accused Brutus of ingratitude in his famous speech at Caesar's funeral. The actual line is: 'Ingratitude, more strong than traitors' arms.'

> ### Evelina
>
> - picking at the coarse food
> - a close bond of understanding and companionship
> - the cheering warmth of her arms
> - She listened as attentively as a mother
> - she put her lips down to his harsh curls
> - Evelina's voice rose clear and true
> - Evelina let out the laughter that had been welling inside her
> - 'Now I going tell you how we'll fix that brute, Mr Chase.'

The plot – conflicts and twists

3 Clement has to stand on the platform in assembly, with a cross drawn on his forehead, and is made to recite a speech on ingratitude in front of 400 pupils. What are your thoughts on:

- Mr Chase's treatment of Clement?
- the idea of forcing children to give money for the Headmaster's leaving present?
- the reasons why Clement is unable to make a contribution?
- the *irony* of a boy like Clement giving money to a man like Mr Megahey?

4 Re-read the final section of the story (from line 217). There are two dramatic 'twists in the tail' here. Work through the twists and ironies by considering the following questions.

a Why exactly is Clement 'turned to stone' (lines 217–8)?

b Why hasn't Clement realised whose house this is until this moment?

c Why doesn't Mr Megahey recognise Clement?

d What is ironic about Mr Megahey giving money to Clement?

e Why does Clement delay handing over the money until on the platform?

f How does Clement manage to 'fix' Mr Chase – as Evelina puts it?

g What makes the ending so satisfying?

Themes – what is it really about?

5 What impressions does Sealy give you of Clement's school? Find evidence in the story to support the statements below.

a The boys are reluctant to attend and live in fear of punishment.

b The teachers are casual, self-important and badly educated themselves.

c The pupils are drilled as if they are in the army.

d The discipline is violent and unfair.

e The teachers enjoy humiliating their pupils.

6 What impressions does Sealy give you of Clement's home? Find evidence to support the following statements.

   a His family has very little to eat.

   b Their home is tiny and run-down.

   c They have very little money to spend.

   d The children have to make do with what they have got.

   e Evelina was unable to carry on with her schooling.

7 The title of the story carries a reminder of the most famous 'pieces of silver' – the thirty pieces paid to Judas Iscariot for betraying Jesus. Can you see any ways in which this story could be about betrayal?

The writer and the writing – Sealy at work

Characterisation

8 You will have noticed from the section on **Characters** that Sealy gives us a stronger impression of Mr Chase and Evelina by deliberately contrasting them with each other. Look closely at the way he contrasts characters in the following examples of description and dialogue. What is the effect of these contrasts?

Contrast one image . . .	. . . with another
Chase his cold eyes (line 44)	**Evelina** the cheering warmth of her arms (line 176)
The boys glanced apprehensively . . . tried feverishly (lines 9–10)	**The teachers** leisurely . . . laughing . . . sauntered (lines 12–13)
Chase a squat jug of a man (line 74)	**Mrs Dovecot** a long thread of a woman whose bones want had picked like an eagle (lines 130–1)
Chase 'Surely our old Head would expire if he knew that in his school he harboured so many thankless Brutuses.' (lines 91–2)	**Mr Dovecot** 'Did yo' hear thet, Maud?...I'll bet you ain't never did.' (lines 164–5)

A closer look at some language choices – Setting

9 Sealy also uses contrast in his description of the different settings in the story. Look closely at the language describing the world of the playground and the school in the opening two paragraphs, and then the changes in the boys as the school day starts. Think about the effect of:

- 'the noisy playfield' **being covered in** 'a pall of silence'
- 'games . . . climbers . . . enjoying' **changing to** assembled . . . inspection . . . file'.

10 Look also at the descriptions of the Dovecots' home (lines 112–33) and of Mr Megahey's home (lines 202–17). How does this contrast help you to understand the unfairness at the heart of the story?

The Red Ball Ismith Khan

Background

Ismith Khan was born in Trinidad in 1925 to an East Indian Muslim family. He grew up in a home overlooking Woodford Square in Port of Spain, which became famous for its huge political rallies during the Trinidad independence campaign. Trinidad was a Spanish, then a British colony for centuries and only achieved full independence in 1962. Both Khan's father and grandfather were strong and determined personalities, and his grandfather had been active in the anti-colonial protests against British rule in India in the 1880s, before the family moved to the West Indies along with thousands of other East Indians. Ismith Khan was educated in Trinidad and then trained in journalism, eventually writing for the *Trinidad Guardian*. He is internationally recognised as the author of three classic novels set in the Caribbean, although he has spent the last thirty years of his life studying, teaching and writing in America, eventually settling in New York.

> **Woodford Square** (line 13): a famous square in the centre of Port of Spain, the capital city of Trinidad, named after Sir Ralph Woodford, a British Governor of Trinidad in the early 19th century. The statue is probably that of Triton, a Greek sea god, believed to cause islands to rise out of the sea.
>
> **Tunapuna** (line 25): a small seaside village, eight miles outside Port of Spain.
>
> **ajoupa hut** (line 49): a small hut made by weaving branches together.

What's the story?

1 List the ten main events in Bolan's life, starting with the move from Tunapuna. The first three have been done for you.

> 1 Bolan and his mother and father move to the city, Port of Spain.
> 2 He goes to the market school and is beaten.
> 3 He watches the boys play cricket in Woodford Square every evening.
> 4 . . .

2 What period of time does the story cover in total and how many evenings does the story describe in detail?

Characters – what are they like?

3 The story revolves around Bolan and his attempts to come to terms with a new way of life in the city. Why do you think Bolan:

- watches the boys playing cricket every night?
- refuses to answer to the names the boys give him?
- touches the powerful-looking statue?
- refuses free black pudding from the vendor?
- takes the money to buy the red ball?
- pays for black pudding for all the boys?

4 Re-read the paragraph beginning 'The same feeling flooded across his heart . . .' (lines 177–82).

    a What is the 'same feeling' that Bolan is experiencing, do you think?

    b What has triggered this feeling again?

    c What has 'released' him from the feeling earlier in the evening?

The plot – conflicts and twists

5 The questions about Bolan above suggest his inner conflict. This leads him to take the money and brings him into conflict with his father. Think about the reasons for this conflict and the way it develops in the following extracts.

    a 'The boy saw him only late in the evenings now, and each evening he brought home a nip of Black Cat rum.' (lines 130–2)

    b 'You beginning to play big shot! You could talk better than you moomah and poopah. Boy! You don't know how lucky you is to be goin' to school. When I was your age . . .' (lines 138–40)

    c He looked like an old man. He let his hair grow on his head and face unless they were going to Tunapuna. (lines 152–4)

    d 'As soon as we did have a li'l money save we have to go and get a . . .' (lines 172–3)

    e 'Is true,' she mumbled, 'that we ain't save much, that you believe you work hard for nothing, but don't forget how much we had to borrow to move to Port of Spain.' (lines 220–2)

    f 'It ain't have no thief in my family . . . we never rob nobody a black cent.' (lines 264–5)

6 Think about the 'twist in the tail' in the final two paragraphs (from line 292).

    a What happens in Bolan's 'dream'?

    b What does Bolan realise about his 'dream' the following morning?

Themes – what is it really about?

7 Which of the following ideas seem to you to be most central to the story? Choose **two** and select details from the story to demonstrate how these themes are explored:

- the suffering which poverty brings
- the need to be loved and appreciated
- the differences between fathers and mothers
- crime and punishment
- the skill of fast bowling
- the difficulty of adapting to a new home.

The writer and the writing – Ismith Khan at work

Characterisation

8 Ismith Khan presents his story almost wholly from Bolan's *point of view*. However, the paragraph beginning 'She took the boy to the standpipe . . .' (line 286) shows us his mother's point of view. What is revealed here about her character and her understanding of her son?

9 We also see Bolan's father largely from Bolan's point of view, but he is not just characterised as a drunken, violent bully. How does Ismith Khan provoke sympathy for the father and suggest that there is more to him than this? Find evidence in the story for the following statements:

a He is just as miserable as Bolan about the move from Tunapuna.

b He has made the move for the sake of his family.

c He is embarrassed by his poverty and lack of education.

d He takes great pride in the honest reputation of his family.

e He works hard but is worried about money and feels a sense of failure.

f He loves his son deeply but finds it difficult to show his feelings.

A closer look at some language choices

10 Ismith Khan suggests the extreme poverty of Bolan's family through the dialogue in which money problems are discussed. How does he suggest this poverty at other points in the story, for example:

a the names which the boys call Bolan at the start of the story

b Bolan's admiration for the cricket set (lines 73–8)

c The 'pipe in the centre of the yard' (line 168) and Bolan's 'mat in the corner' (line 204).

11 Re-read the paragraph beginning 'It was turning that salmon and orange light . . .' (line 116). What is suggested about Bolan's new home and his feelings about it in this description? Look closely at words like 'tunnelled . . . deep backyard . . . last barrack-room . . . high wall . . .' as you consider your response.

12 As a contrast with the grimness and unhappiness, Ismith Khan describes moments of real joy for Bolan. Look at the description of his bowling (lines 89–100).

a Which words and *similes* suggest the grace and power of his bowling?

b Why does Khan choose the word 'sang' in the final sentence of the story?

13 Finally, Ismith Khan describes the giant green statue at the start of the story and then reminds us of it at the end, as if it is an important *symbol* of something. Re-read the description of the statue (lines 17–22) and then decide:

• why you think the statue is important to Bolan

• why the statue merges with his father at the end.

The Young Couple Ruth Prawer Jhabvala

Background

Ruth Prawer Jhabvala was born in Germany in 1927, the daughter of Polish-Jewish parents, who emigrated to England to escape persecution before the start of the Second World War in 1939. She obtained a degree in Literature from London University and then, after meeting and marrying an Indian architect, Cyrus Jhabvala, in 1951, she emigrated again, to New Delhi, India, where they raised three daughters. Since 1955 she has become internationally famous for her nine novels, three volumes of short stories and her film adaptations and screenplays. Her novel *Heat and Dust* won the prestigious Booker Prize in 1975 and her filmed adaptation of it won a BAFTA for Best Screenplay. She won Oscars for her adaptations of two E.M. Forster novels, *A Room With a View* and *Howards End*, and was nominated for another Oscar for her adaptation of Kazuo Ishiguro's *The Remains of the Day*. Much of the writing in her novels and stories is concerned with the culture clash between the Indian and the British ways of life.

What's the story?

1 **The Young Couple** is the story of a marriage which begins in England, the wife's home country, and then moves to the husband's home in India. Take a large piece of paper and trace the feelings of the young wife, Cathy, as the relationship develops, entering further stages on the graph below. Estimate the passage of time along the bottom. Should it be days, weeks, months, or even years?

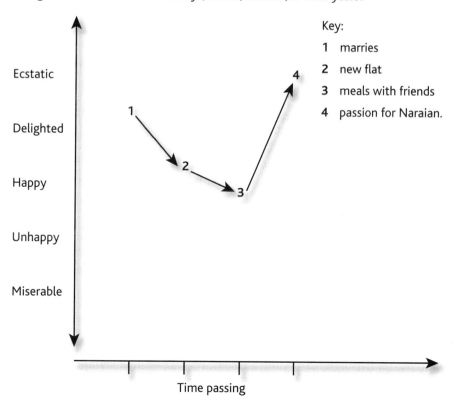

Key:
1 marries
2 new flat
3 meals with friends
4 passion for Naraian.

Ecstatic

Delighted

Happy

Unhappy

Miserable

Time passing

Characters – what are they like?

2 How would you describe Cathy? Is she independent, determined, loving or lazy, ungrateful, discontented – or is she all of these at different points in the story?

3 How would you describe Naraian? Is he idealistic, determined, loving or is he weak, dependent, selfish – or is he all of these at different points?

4 How would you describe Naraian's parents? Are they interfering, possessive and bossy or are they devoted, generous and unselfish – or are they all of these at different points?

Support your impressions of each by referring to their words and actions.

The plot – conflicts and twists

5 Conflicts develop between Cathy and Naraian's family, and eventually between Cathy and Naraian. Trace the pattern of these conflicts (and the changes in Naraian) by answering the following questions:

  a Why doesn't Cathy enjoy the Sunday lunches (line 119)?
  b Why does Cathy feel 'let down' (line 244)?
  c What does Naraian mean by 'It's not Oxford Street, you know' (line 274)?
  d Why does Cathy feel 'very miserable' (line 389)?
  e Why is Cathy annoyed that 'Naraian did not come to the defence of their nest . . .' (lines 440–1)?

6 One of the central *narrative* questions is: **Will the young couple lose their happy independence and become completely dominated by Naraian's family?** What are your feelings about this by the end of the story? Think about:

  • Naraian telling Cathy not to roam naked around the flat (lines 459–60)
  • the sacking of their old sweeper-woman (lines 466–70)
  • Cathy's vision of the room in the final sentence.

Themes – what is it really about?

Culture clash

7 There is a contrast in this story between the life Cathy remembers in England and her new life in India, largely because of differences in customs and beliefs, and particularly in attitudes to women. Identify the differences between the two cultures, as suggested in the story, with reference to the following:

  • the way in which Naraian's friends react to Cathy (lines 52–65)
  • Naraian's behaviour with Cathy in public (lines 66–81)
  • the family's involvement in the young couple's life (lines 139–70)
  • the reasons why Cathy doesn't go out to work (lines 178–94)
  • the attitude of the family to Cathy's shopping trips (lines 216–32).

The tyranny of family domination

8 Despite their best intentions, the young couple are drawn into and dominated by the family. How do Naraian's parents establish control? Think about:

- the payment for the flat
- the pressure to attend family meals (lines 119–26)
- the comments on Cathy's behaviour (lines 231–2)
- the reasons why Naraian finally accepts a job in the family business
- the family criticism of the flat (lines 429–37)
- the reasons why Naraian finally wants to move into the family home.

The writer and the writing – Jhabvala at work

Characterisation

9 Most of this story is told from Cathy's *point of view*, for example, her view of Naraian's friends: 'She didn't care for . . . she thought . . . what galled her . . . she felt . . . felt slighted . . . saw . . .' (lines 53–63). Also look at lines 376–91 where Cathy gradually realises that Naraian has accepted the job with the family firm without discussing it with her. Why do you think Jhabvala gives us Cathy's point of view here? Does this technique:

- make us share her feelings and sympathise with her
- make us share Cathy's standpoint as an outsider
- build up suspense, in that we know as little as she does about the job?

10 You have considered your response to Naraian in the section on **Characters**. Jhabvala reveals his character to us (and the way it changes) in subtle, indirect ways rather than telling us precisely what to think. What does she suggest about Naraian in the following descriptions of his expressions and gestures?

a . . . she looked again towards Naraian who was now busy eating the flesh around the stone of his mango . . . (lines 238–9).

b He looked at her out of the corner of his eye, then decided to be bold: turned out the light . . . (lines 275–6).

c Cathy caught Naraian's eye again; he looked away quickly . . . (lines 388–9).

d . . . he kicked a door so that its poor, cheap wood splintered a bit further . . . (lines 481–2).

A closer look at language choices

11 How does Jhabvala suggest the family's power and control over the couple in:

- the descriptions of the food, the furniture, the parents . . . (lines 129–38), in the description of the garden (lines 372–5) and in the final sentence
- the water imagery (lines 140–1)
- the image of the 'ring' (line 197)?

12 How does Jhabvala give the impression that the relationship between the young couple and the family is like a battle? Look at lines 439–49?

four rupees (line 21): The rupee is the Indian unit of currency. At today's rates, four rupees are worth about six pence.

Leela's Friend R. K. Narayan

Background

Rasipuram Krishnaswamy Narayanaswamy was born in the Indian city of Madras in 1906 and, apart from occasional trips abroad, lived in India all his life. His father was the headmaster of a local school. Narayan trained to be a journalist and then went on to win international recognition for his numerous novels, five collections of short stories, four collections of essays and two travel books. He was admired and encouraged by the English novelist Graham Greene, who described him as 'the foremost Indian writer in English' and suggested that he should shorten his name for publication purposes. He is widely regarded as the finest Anglo-Indian writer of the twentieth century. He has received several awards and his work has been translated into many different languages. **Leela's Friend** is one of his best-known and most popular short stories. Narayan died in May 2001, aged ninety-four.

What's the story?

1 After your first reading, fix the story in your mind by identifying seven more main events and listing them in order.

> 1 Mr and Mrs Sivasanker decide to employ Sidda.
> 2 . . .

Characters – what are they like?

2 What is your view of Sidda, the servant boy? Is he a suitable 'friend' for Leela? Do you accept the following evidence against him?

a He is vague about his previous employer. (lines 9–14).

b He makes false claims about the moon and misleads Leela (lines 41–57).

c He is uneducated and illiterate. (lines 63–70)

d He looks guilty at the mention of the chain and then runs away (lines 93–9).

e Mrs Sivasanker thinks of him as a 'villain' (line 113).

f He has a criminal record for stealing jewellery from children (lines 125–7).

g The Inspector calls him a 'devil' (line 151).

h Mrs Sivasanker calls him a 'rough fellow' (line 172).

What evidence can you select from the story to give a more sympathetic view of Sidda's character?

3 What is your view of Leela's parents? Are they good parents? Look at the following evidence in their favour and decide whether you agree. Then identify evidence which is less sympathetic.

a They are generous with their daughter (like the gift of the gold chain).

b They provide her with a companion, with books, catalogues, pencils (line 60).

c They are very concerned for the safety of their daughter (lines 112–14).

4 Finally, what is your view of Leela? Is she just a spoilt, thoughtless, bossy and rather naïve five-year-old – or is there more to her than this? Identify evidence from the story for both views of Leela.

The plot – conflicts and twists

There is a clear conflict between Leela's view of Sidda and her parents' view of him. The central *narrative* question is **'Did Sidda steal the gold chain?'** (or who is right about him – Leela or her parents)?

5 Re-read the section (lines 24–84) which describes the times that Sidda and Leela spend together. Narayan shares this with the reader but not Leela's parents. What is there in these lines that might convince you to share Leela's trust in Sidda?

6 Re-read the final section (line 175 to the end). How many twists and *ironies* and injustices can you find here?

Themes – what is it really about?

7 The honesty, directness and wisdom of children can often expose the stupidity and unfairness of the adult world, and many writers make use of this irony. Look at extracts a–d below, and decide what Narayan might be suggesting through Leela about:

- prejudice
- poverty
- class divisions
- injustice
- being a good parent
- what is important in life and what isn't.

a 'I don't like you, Mother. You are always abusing and worrying Sidda. Why are you so rough?'
   'But he has taken away your chain . . .'
   'Let him. It doesn't matter. Tell me a story.' (lines 103–6)

b 'Why should not Sidda sit in our chair, Mother?' Mother didn't answer the question. Leela said a moment later, 'Sidda is gone because he wouldn't be allowed to sleep inside the house just as we do. Why should he always be made to sleep outside the house, Mother? I think he is angry with us, Mother.' (lines 118–23)

c 'He is a thief. He has taken away your gold chain.'
   'Let him. I will have a new chain,' Leela said, and all of them laughed. (lines 139–41)

d Leela felt disgusted with the whole business and said, 'Leave him alone, he hasn't taken the chain.'
   'You are not at all a reliable prosecution witness, my child,' observed the inspector humorously. (lines 154–8)

The writer and the writing – Narayan at work

Characterisation – the presentation of Sidda

8 In the **Characters** section, you considered some harsh judgements of Sidda, mainly from the *point of view* of the adults in the story. In the **Plot** section, you looked at the time Sidda spent with Leela in order to consider a more sympathetic view of him. Now look at other ways in which Narayan encourages the reader to take a sympathetic view of Sidda and the life he leads. Look at the effect of:

- the way Narayan has Sidda address Mr Sivasanker in the opening section
- the way Narayan lists his jobs (lines 22–3)
- the way Narayan positions him in the house: 'She made him squat on the floor…' (line 61), 'He sat down on the floor near the bed . . .' (line 77)
- the description 'that good fellow' (line 69). Whose view is this?
- Sidda's response to the accusations: 'His throat went dry. He blinked and answered that he did not know' (lines 93–4); 'Sidda stood with bowed head' (lines 134–5); 'He looked at her mutely, like an animal' (line 166).

9 Look at the contrast Narayan builds up between Leela's feelings for Sidda and her feelings for her parents. Find evidence for the following statements in the story.

a Sidda makes time to play very patiently with Leela, to excite her imagination, to read her stories and to answer her questions.

b Leela's parents may give her material things, but they give her no time or attention, they blame her, laugh at her, fail to answer her questions and discipline her too harshly and angrily.

c Leela finds joy in the company of Sidda and is deeply unhappy when he is accused and eventually removed.

A closer look at some language choices

10 One of the suggested themes in the **Themes** section is prejudice. Sidda certainly suffers from the way the adults form snap judgements based on appearances or on rumour. How does Narayan draw attention to this prejudging or prejudice:

- in the opening twenty lines
- in Mrs Sivasanker's instant suspicions (lines 91–3)
- in her disturbed thoughts (lines 110–14)
- in Mr Sivasanker's final description of Sidda (line 194)?

Games at Twilight Anita Desai

Background

Anita Desai was born Anita Mazumdar to an Indian father and German mother near New Delhi, India, in 1937 and spoke German at home, Hindi with her friends and English at school, Her first story was published when she was only seven years old. She graduated from Delhi University in 1957 with an English Literature degree and married businessman Ashvin Desai in 1958. She had four children and began writing seriously while they were still very young. Her novels and stories often explore the tensions within family life and many have been written for children. She has also taught in England and the USA. She received the Guardian Award for children's fiction for the novel, *The Village by the Sea* (1982) and the 1978 National Academy of Letters Award for the novel, *Fire on the Mountain* (1977).

> **bougainvillea** (line 20): a brightly coloured climbing plant which only grows in hot climates.
>
> **croton** (line 90): tropical shrub.
>
> **jamun** (line 167): fruit from the 'rose-apple' tree, which originated in India and now grows throughout Asia.
>
> **laurels** (line 187): a wreath of laurel leaves was traditionally worn as a symbol of victory and honour.

What's the story?

1 Think about the range of feelings Ravi experiences in the course of this afternoon. Describe how he is feeling at each of the following points in the story, e.g. when his mother keeps him indoors, Ravi feels trapped, confined, frustrated.

a He is allowed out.

b He is not chosen to be It.

c He hears Raghu whistling.

d He looks for a hiding-place.

e He can't reach the garage key.

f He enters the shed and avoids capture.

g He takes in his surroundings.

h The spider tickles his neck.

i He thinks about winning the game.

j He flings himself at the pillar and bawls, 'Den!'.

k He charges the other children and bawls, 'I won'.

l Mira puts him 'at the end of the line'.

m He lies down on the damp grass.

Characters – what are they like?

2 There are a lot of children in this story – brothers, sisters and cousins – and, as in many families, there appears to be a clear hierarchy (or pecking order) as the children compete for attention. Concentrate on Ravi, Raghu, Mira and Manu.

    a Who do you think is the eldest?

    b Who do you think is the youngest?

    c What do you learn about their size and appearance?

    d What do you learn about their characters and relationships with other children?

The plot – conflicts and twists

3 Re-read the story and find the key points where conflict and suspense are built up. What builds the tension in the following moments?

    a 'The children, too, felt released. They too began tumbling, shoving, pushing against each other . . .' (lines 36–7) . . . 'The shoves became harder. Some kicked out. The motherly Mira intervened. She pulled the boys roughly apart. There was a tearing sound of cloth but it was lost in the heavy panting and angry grumbling . . .' (lines 45–8).

    b Raghu's counting (line 71), 'blood-curdling yell' (line 75); whistling (lines 81, 115–16); crashing around (line 116); and stick-whacking (lines 124–5).

    c Ravi's glimpse of Raghu's legs (lines 89–90).

    d The growing dark (line 193) and the growing silence (line 176).

4 The central *narrative* question in this story could be **Will Ravi win the game?**

    a Why is winning the game so important to Ravi?

    b What is the cruel twist at the end of the game?

    c How does the ending of the story (from line 256) represent a complete reversal for Ravi and all his hopes?

Themes – what is it really about?

5 Choose **two** ideas from the following list which you feel are the most central to the story. Support your selections with details and quotations from the story.

    a Childhood is not always a happy and innocent time.

    b Childhood play is a serious business.

    c It's very difficult being the youngest or smallest in the family.

    d Sibling rivalry can be fierce and competitive.

    e Young children are always desperate to be older and bigger.

    f Life is very short and death awaits us all.

    g The most important thing in life (and death) is to be remembered.

    h Individuals don't really matter in the great scheme of things.

6 Arthur Miller, the American playwright, once wrote about the image in his mind as he sat down to write *Death of a Salesman*, one of his best-known plays:

> . . . the image of a need greater than hunger or sex or thirst, a need to leave a thumbprint somewhere on the world; a need for immortality, and by admitting it, the knowing that one has carefully inscribed one's name on a cake of ice on a hot July day.

Can you see the connection between Miller's ideas and the sad lesson which Ravi learns?

The writer and the writing – Desai at work

Characterisation

7 Much of the story concentrates on Ravi. Look again at the paragraph beginning 'Ravi heard the whistling . . .' (line 83). Why does Desai:

- make us share Ravi's *point of view* ('he heard . . . he felt . . . had a frightening glimpse . . . looked about him.')
- contrast Ravi's legs with Raghu's
- ask us the question 'Where could he burrow?'
- refer to nose-picking and snot?

A closer look at some language choices

This is a very descriptive story, but Desai's descriptions (of the weather, of the garden, of the shed) are not just there to 'set the scene'. As you look at the following sections of writing, think about how Desai might be choosing language and descriptive detail to underline key ideas in the story.

Images of life, time and death

8 Why does Desai describe the children bursting out from the house at the start of the story as 'like seeds from a crackling, over-ripe pod' (lines 14–15)?

9 How are the ideas of death and lifelessness emphasised in lines 24 to 31?

10 Why does Desai have Raghu say to Manu, 'You're dead'?

11 Why does Desai describe Ravi's hiding place as a 'depressing mortuary' (lines 113-114) which has 'a muffled smell, as of graves' (lines 127–8)?

12 Why does Desai emphasise the growing darkness, coolness and colourlessness of the 'twilight' in lines 193–202 and throughout the final section?

13 Why is the chant in line 228 introduced and then given in full in lines 252–5?

14 Desai describes the final game as 'funereal' (line 259). What descriptive details give the impression of a funeral in the final section (lines 249 to the end)?

Images of violence

15 Why does Desai write of Manu's reappearance that it is 'as if he had dropped out of an invisible cloud or from a bird's claws . . .' (lines 67–8)?

16 Why does Desai write that Raghu 'stalked off in search of worthier prey'? (lines 80–1) and repeat the idea in line 125?

The Winter Oak Yuri Nagibin

Background

Yuri Nagibin was born in Russia in 1920. He trained to be a journalist but became respected for a wide range of writing, including film scripts, biographies and short stories. He wrote the screenplay for *The Chairman*, which has become one of Russian cinema's most important films and he wrote a book about Yuri Gagarin, the world's first spaceman, entitled *Gagarin's Smile*. It is for his short stories that he is best known, however, and he has been compared to Anton Chekhov, the great Russian dramatist and master of the short story form. Nagibin's stories are often concerned with rural village life, and he is particularly admired for his sympathetic treatment of his characters and his beautiful descriptions of the natural world. He was married to the poet Bella Akhmadulina in 1960. He died in April 1994. *The Winter Oak* is translated from the original Russian.

What's the story?

1 The story has two locations – the school and the forest – and covers one working day in the life of a teacher, Anna Vasilevna. What is she most likely to remember about the events of this day? Add five more main events for each location.

School	Forest
1 Begins teaching parts of speech	1 Savushkin shows her elk tracks.
2 . . .	2 . . .

2 There are two flashbacks involving the school. What does Anna remember about her teaching in the previous year and her conversation with the geography mistress?

Characters – what are they like?

3 The story has two main characters, Anna Vasilevna and Savushkin. At the end of the school section (line 133), what do you think is Anna's view of Savushkin? Write some notes on Savushkin, as if you are Anna at this point in the story. You should include how Anna's impressions of Savushkin have changed by the end of the story and also consider:

- Savushkin's lateness
- his performance in class
- impressions of his character
- impressions of his home-life.

4 Think about the following statements about Anna's character and teaching methods. Find references in the school section (up to line 113) to support them. Do you agree with all of them?

a Anna is hard-working, dedicated and serious about teaching.

b She is a young and inexperienced teacher who thinks she is doing better than she actually is.

c She doesn't really know her pupils or understand the lives they lead.

d She jumps to conclusions about the children she teaches.

e She teaches dull subjects which don't touch the lives of her pupils.

f She corrects their language but doesn't always listen to what her pupils are saying.

g She is keen for her lessons to go well and for her pupils to succeed at school.

5 How do your impressions of Anna, as a teacher and as a character, change once you have read the whole story?

The plot – conflicts and twists

6 In the school section, the plot appears to be based on the conflict between a dedicated teacher and a difficult pupil, building up to a showdown with the boy's mother. However, the plot changes direction in the forest section. Place the following extracts in context and trace the reversals, twists and *ironies*.

a The paragraph beginning: 'An elk has been here,' said Savushkin . . . (lines 154-–8).

b 'Look, the ice is so thin . . .' (line 191) to . . . and looking around him (line 197).

c Anna Vasilevna was gazing with delighted interest . . . (line 247–8) to . . . she had walked into a trap (line 252).

d 'Well, Savushkin, thank you for the walk . . .' (line 270) to . . . he was afraid of telling a lie (line 274–5).

e He was guarding his teacher from afar. (lines 289–90).

Themes – what is it really about?

7 Do you think this is a story in which the teacher learns the lessons? Which one of the following lessons seems to you to be most central to the story? Support your decision with detail and quotation from the story.

a Prejudice – it's important not to judge people until you have got to know them by sharing their experiences.

b Education – learning through experience is more effective and enjoyable than academic study in the classroom.

c Language – language is an important and beautiful means of expressing our feelings and should not be reduced to a series of dull classroom exercises.

d Self-knowledge – it's important to admit your mistakes and to learn from them.

e Nature – you should take time out from your busy daily routines to appreciate the beauty of the natural world.

f Poverty – it's possible to be poor in material terms, but rich in your appreciation of the world around you.

The writer and the writing – Nagibin at work

Characterisation

8 We see most of the story from Anna's *point of view*. How does Nagibin suggest to us that her view is often mistaken? Identify use of the *irony* in the following extracts.

 a And she remembered too how she used to be tormented by a ridiculous fear that perhaps they would not understand her. (lines 14–16).

 b She felt sad and confused as she always did when faced with a child telling lies. (lines 117–18)

A closer look at some language choices

9 Re-read the section (lines 79–93) where Nagibin first introduces the oak tree.
 a Why does he introduce the tree at this point?

 b How does he show its importance to Savushkin?

 c How does he show Anna's failure to understand this importance?

10 Re-read the sentence (lines 207–8) which describes Anna's first encounter with the oak: 'In the middle of the glade, clothed in glittering white raiment, huge and majestic as a cathedral, stood an oak.'

 a Why does Nagibin hold back the word 'oak' until the end of the sentence?

 b How does he suggest that this tree has special significance?

 c What is the effect of *personifying* the oak here and elsewhere?

11 How does Nagibin give the impression that the forest and the oak belong to a separate and magical world, which keeps its secrets covered up and will only gradually reveal them? Why is this idea central to the story? Look at descriptions of the oak, like: '. . . covered with a thick white blanket of snow . . . imprisoned in an armour of clear ice . . .' (lines 165–7).

Overview

OPENING WORLDS

Thinking and linking

Bringing the stories together

The exam questions will invite you to refer to more than one story, so you need to do some grouping of the stories as part of your revision. The questions are likely to focus on thematic links between the stories, for example, similar problems, conflicts, ways of life. Remember that for **English**, Unit 2, you only have to work on **six** stories (the first six until January 2006, and the final six from then on). For **English Literature** you need to work on all the stories in **Opening Worlds**.

Two Kinds: America. Pushy Chinese mother. Piano lessons – disastrous competition. Arguments. Later - Ni kan (30+) given piano. Mother dies. N. plays piano. Reaches understanding.

Stage 1

First, write a summary in note form to remind you of each story. Aim for about twenty words per story, as in the example in the margin.

Stage 2

Give each story a new title that helps to remind you of its key themes. You could use a phrase from the story, for example:

- **Dead Men's Path**: 'Let the Hawk Perch and Let the Eagle Perch'
- **The Young Couple**: 'The Tyranny of Family Domination'.

Stage 3

Construct a mind-map like the one shown below. Map out all the stories' titles and all the links you are able to make between them.

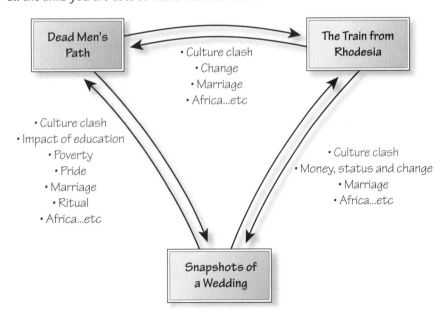

Stage 4

Try to group the stories under broad thematic headings. For example, stories with a theme, and therefore under a heading of Family relationships, might include:

- Snapshots of a Wedding
- The Gold-Legged Frog
- Two Kinds
- The Tall Woman and...
- Pieces of Silver
- The Red Ball
- The Young Couple
- Leela's Friend
- Games At Twilight

Can you see why each story has been selected? Would you add any others?

The same or different stories might have a theme and be listed under the following headings:

- the world of the child
- culture clashes
- unfairness
- poverty
- school
- fitting in.

Do you need to extend the headings to include more themes or to make the headings more precise (e.g. Theft, Humiliation, Corporal punishment)?

Stage 5

You can also establish links between the ways in which the stories are written. This is more difficult, but you will gain more marks in the exam if you can make a connection between the styles of different writers and the effects they achieve.

As you go back over the stories and through your notes, remind yourself of the stories which use:

- a particular character's *point of view*
- flashbacks, time shifts and long time spans
- *contrasts* – of characters, dialogue, settings
- suspense and unexpected twists
- *symbolic* details
- striking descriptions of setting or of physical appearance
- a particular *tone* – chatty, serious, humorous, ironic, angry
- a particular mood – *pathos* (feelings of sadness), triumph, disappointment
- hopeful endings, unhappy endings, unresolved endings.

Examination preparation

Sample Questions
English, Unit 2: Different Cultures, Section A

Foundation Tier

Either

1 Choose **two** stories from **Opening Worlds** where the characters behave in ways that you find surprising or unexpected. What is there in each story you have chosen which helps to explain this surprising or unexpected behaviour?

Or

2 Read the extract from **The Tall Woman and Her Short Husband** (from line 224, 'The success of a meeting . . .' to line 264 '. . . and he won't have any money.'), and then answer the question below.

Some readers might feel that Mrs Tall and Mr Short, in **The Tall Woman and Her Short Husband,** and the daughter in **Two Kinds** are treated unkindly. Write about what happens in the two stories that seems unkind or unfair.

In your answer refer to:

- why the characters behave as they do
- the importance of the time and/or place in which the stories are set.

Higher Tier

Either

1 Write about **two** stories from **Opening Worlds** in which older or traditional ways of life are affected by change. What is the effect on the characters involved, and their community, and how is this shown in the stories?

Or

2 Read the extract from **The Tall Woman and Her Short Husband** (line 224 to line 284), then answer the question below.

Write about the way in which particular characters in **The Tall Woman and Her Short Husband** and in **one other** story from this collection are put under pressure by other members of the community in which they live. Why is this pressure exerted, and how are its consequences shown in the stories?

Sample Questions
English Literature,
Unit 2: Prose Post-1914

Foundation Tier

Either

1. Read the extract from **The Red Ball** (line 152, 'His father then fell . . .' to line 233 '. . . went back to sleep again.') and then answer the question below.

Both **The Red Ball** and **The Gold-Legged Frog** show families struggling against poverty.
- How are the families affected by this struggle against poverty?
- What do you find particularly moving about the presentation of the struggle against poverty in each story?

Or

2. Write about **two stories** from **Opening Worlds** in which schools seem to be out of touch with their pupils or their communities.
- In what ways are the schools out of touch?
- How do the writers make clear to you the differences between life in school and life out of school?

Or

3. Choose **two stories** from **Opening Worlds** which you feel show unhappy relationships between parents and children.
- In what ways are the relationships unhappy?
- Do the stories lead you to blame someone or something for the unhappiness?

Higher Tier

Either

1. Read the extract from **The Red Ball** (line 152 'His father then fell . . .' to line 233 '. . . went back to sleep again.') and then answer the question below.

Explore the ways in which a family's struggle against poverty is presented in **The Red Ball** and **one other** story from **Opening Worlds**. How do Khan and the other writer make you aware of the suffering which poverty can bring to a family?

Or

2. Explore the ways in which **two stories** from **Opening Worlds** present schools which are out of touch with their pupils or their communities. How do the writers contrast the world of the school with the world outside in these two stories?

Or

3. Explore **two stories** from **Opening Worlds** which you feel present unhappy relationships between parents and children. How do the writers make you feel the force of this unhappiness and understand the reasons behind it?

The style of the exam questions

- All questions require you to be familiar with **two** linked stories but you won't have to compare the stories.
- All questions will focus on the social, cultural, historical and literary contexts of the stories.
- The style of the questions for English and for English Literature is more or less the same. You have a choice of **two** questions in English, and **three** in English Literature. You have slightly longer for your English Literature answer (**45 minutes** compared with **40 minutes** for English) but you have to prepare all **twelve** stories (compared with **six** for English). Your English answer on the stories is worth **10%** of your overall mark for English; your English Literature answer is worth **25%** of your overall English Literature mark.
- Questions may use an extract from one of the stories as a starting-point.
- Questions are often addressed to 'you' as an individual with a personal response.

What are the examiners looking for?

1. **Relevance**: you must answer the question they have set.
2. **Response**: you must express **your view** of the stories in relation to the question.
3. **Textual detail**: you must support your response with direct quotation and detail from the stories.
4. **Evaluation**: you must try to look closely at the way the stories are written.
5. **Expression**: you must make sure that you express your ideas clearly and accurately. In English Literature, for instance, **5%** of your mark will depend on your control of spelling, punctuation and sentence structure.

If you keep these **five** areas in mind as you plan and write your answers, you will cover all the important **Assessment Objectives** and achieve a good mark.

How does this work in practice?

Look back at Sample Question 1 (English Literature, Higher Tier) on page 180 and the passage from **The Red Ball**. Then read the following extract taken from a sample answer to the question. Keep the **five** areas in mind and decide whether this candidate, John, is giving the examiners what they want.

> Ismith Khan makes me aware that Bolan's father in particular suffers from feelings of failure, disappointment and guilt because of their poor lifestyle. It was his decision to move the family to the city and so he tries desperately to keep up appearances when he returns to Tunapuna. He has a shave and a trim and boasts 'that he was making three dollars a day at the American base.' This boast is very different from the 'small noise' he makes later when he faces the reality that they only have eight shillings saved in the can. Ismith Khan's description of his appearance as an 'old man' who 'let his hair grow on his head and face' suggests suffering, failure and defeat.

Examiner comments

General features

The answer makes use of the extract from **The Red Ball**, selecting relevant detail and quoting from it directly. John shows awareness of the question's focus on poverty and displays some personal response to the plight of the family. He makes a case for sympathising with Bolan's father, which is not a simple or obvious approach to this story or this question. John sees that the father is more than just a drunken bully.

Detailed commentary

1 **Relevance:** John focuses on the exact wording of the question in his opening sentence, which makes the direction and relevance of his argument clear.

2 **Response:** He also makes his personal responses to Bolan's father and his poverty clear from the start (*makes me aware…failure, disappointment and guilt*).

3 **Textual detail:** He then supports his responses with textual evidence by referring to key details (*his decision to move the family…*) and by using brief quotations neatly integrated into his sentences.

4 **Evaluation:** The most impressive thing of all, however, is that John shows an awareness of the writer at work and he comments fully on the quotations he selects. He refers to Ismith Khan directly, evaluates the effect of his descriptions of the father's appearance and points out and comments on the effect of the contrast in the father's public and private faces.

5 **Expression:** John expresses himself very fluently and accurately.

Work of this quality should bring John an **A* grade** overall.

Model answer

One of the reasons for John's success is that he remembers the **three-point formula** and he uses this structure very skilfully (see poetry section, page 134).

> ### Three-point formula
>
> - **Respond** (make a relevant point)
>   the 'father's feelings of failure'.
>
> - **Quote** (support the point with quotation from the text)
>   the 'small noise'.
>
> - **Comment** (evaluate the effect of the writing in the quotation)
>   contrast 'with boast . . . the reality of poverty'.

Coursework

English Literature, Scheme B

Unit 7: Coursework

If you are following Scheme B you could choose to submit coursework based on the stories in **Opening Worlds**. A single piece of coursework, comparing two stories from **Opening Worlds**, could cover both the comparative and contextual requirements in one go. You also have a free choice of which stories to cover (unlike in the exam), so you can go for your favourites.

Ideas for possible coursework tasks

1. Compare the presentation of school life in **The Pieces of Silver** and **The Winter Oak**. How do Sealy and Nagibin suggest to you that the schools in these two stories are out of touch with the needs of their pupils? (*Includes both the comparative and contextual elements.*)

2. Good short stories often build to a surprising ending. Compare the ways in which Nadine Gordimer (in **The Train From Rhodesia**) and Chinua Achebe (in **Dead Men's Path**) give the reader a 'twist in the tail'. What is the effect of the two endings on your understanding and enjoyment of each story? (*Includes both the comparative and contextual elements.*)

3. If you want to be a bit more adventurous, you could always tackle a task which combines your favourite story/stories with other texts and other genres. As we have seen, the stories in **Opening Worlds** touch on many themes (poverty, family conflict, the world of the child . . .) which could tie in with your reading of other post-1914 prose texts, as well as with your reading of post-1914 drama and poetry. The 'Generations' section of the **Opening Lines** poetry collection, for instance, could offer some interesting pairings:

   - **Follower** (Seamus Heaney) and **The Red Ball** – look at father–son relationships?
   - **I Remember, I Remember** (Philip Larkin) and **Games at Twilight** – look at feelings of insignificance?

English Literature, Scheme B

Unit 8: Exam instead of Coursework

You could also use **Opening Worlds** as your prose text for the exam alternative to coursework if your school chooses to follow this route. There will be a choice of **two** questions (as in English, Unit 2) and you have to study **all twelve** stories (as in English Literature, Unit 2).

Biographies of the poets

(All page references to the poems are to **Opening Lines** anthology)

(Pre-1914)

Herbert Asquith (**The Volunteer**, p.34) 1852–1928. Elected to Parliament in 1886. Became Prime Minister in 1909. Criticised for opposing votes for women and for his weak leadership during the Great War. Resigned in 1916 after the disastrous Battle of the Somme.

William Barnes (**Woak Hill**, p.26) 1801–86. A largely self-educated countryman who became a schoolmaster and parson. Best-known for his Dorset dialect poems which depict nature and country people and life with freshness, humour and affection.

William Blake (**The Sick Rose**, p.18, **A Poison Tree**, p.30, **London**, p.56) 1757–1827. Engraver, painter and hugely influential poet, Blake was a Londoner acutely aware of political and religious oppression and of the suffering of the poor. His **Songs of Innocence and Experience** are particularly admired for their powerfully symbolic and vivid imagery.

Elizabeth Barrett Browning (**Sonnet**, p.11) 1806–61. Survived a childhood spinal injury, delicate health and the attentions of a domineering father to elope with poet, Robert Browning, and to forge one of the happiest and most celebrated of literary marriages. The sequence of sonnets, dedicated to her husband, is considered to be her greatest achievement.

Anne Brontë (**Song**, p.41) 1820–49. The youngest and least famous of the three Brontë sisters. Produced two novels (*Agnes Grey* and *The Tenant of Wildfell Hall*) alongside her poetry, in her short, sheltered and troubled life.

Lord Byron (**The Destruction of Sennacherib**, p.37) 1788–1824. His poetry may not be as well regarded as other Romantic poets like Keats or Shelley, but his life and passionate love affairs have become legendary. 'Byronic' has come to mean 'wild, romantic, mysterious'. Died abroad fighting for Greek independence.

Arthur Hugh Clough (**The Latest Decalogue**, p.28) 1819–61. A pupil at the famous Rugby school and a promising scholar. He was plagued by religious doubts and uncertainties, reflected in the satirical and questioning style of many of his poems.

Mary Coleridge (**The Poison Flower**, p.30) 1861–1907. Poet and novelist. Published five novels and four books of poetry, despite caring for ailing parents. Poems tinged with melancholy. The great-great-niece of poet S. T. Coleridge.

William Collins (**Ode, Written in the Beginning of the Year**, p.42) 1721–59. English poet who wrote mainly melancholy odes on nature subjects. Personifies abstract ideas with allegorical effect. Died penniless and insane.

Walter de la Mare (**The Listeners**, p.23) 1873–1956. Poet and novelist, interested in childhood, dreams, nature and tales of mystery. Wrote for both adults and children.

Sydney Dobell (**Tommy's Dead**, p.40) 1824–74 English poet and critic. Wrote long, dramatic poems, but is better known for his shorter ballads.

John Donne (**The Sun Rising**, p.8) 1572–1631. From a wealthy Catholic background. Travelled widely. Fought against the Spanish with Sir Walter Ralegh. Became an MP. A great lover of women in his youth, he was disgraced by a secret marriage in 1601 but later became dean of St Paul's Cathedral and a famous preacher. The first and greatest of the *metaphysical* poets and an original, honest, powerful love poet.

Michael Drayton (**Since there's no help...** , p.16) 1563–1631. Born in Warwickshire, Drayton experimented with a huge variety of poetic forms, including the Shakespearian love sonnet. Died in poverty but buried in Westminster Abbey.

Anne Finch (**The Unequal Fetters**, p.12) 1661–1720. This Countess of Winchilsea was one of the earliest published women poets in England and is often described as the best English female poet prior to the 19th century. Enjoyed a happy marriage to Heneage Finch but could be highly critical of conventional male attitudes.

Dora Greenwell (**A Scherzo A Shy Person's Wishes**, p.13) 1821–82. Dorothy (or Dora) was born in Northumberland and spent a life of quiet service, helping the poor and visiting convicts in Durham prison. She loved the countryside and was deeply interested in theology, writing hymns alongside her poetry. She was a friend of poet Christina Rossetti, and campaigned for better education and votes for women.

Thomas Hardy (**The Ruined Maid**, p.10, **On the Departure Platform**, p.17, **The Darkling Thrush**, p.27, **The Man He Killed**, p.42, **Beeny Cliff**, p.48) 1840–1928. Dorset novelist and poet. Published 11 major novels in 24 years but concentrated on poetry after *Jude the Obscure* shocked readers of the 1890s and was savaged by critics. Deeply affected by his loss of faith in God and by the death of his first wife, he was sharply aware of Victorian hypocrisy, failed love, time and life's tragic ironies. His poetry was original and varied, often colloquial and rooted in his rural background.

Robert Herrick (**Upon Julia's Clothes**, p.8, **To the Virgins, to Make Much of Time**, p.25, **Dreams**, p.31) 1591–1674. A country clergyman, famous for his love poetry which was often transformed into popular songs and called 'lyrics'. A happy rather than a passionate love poet.

Thomas Hood (**Faithless Sally Brown**, p.14, **I Remember, I Remember**, p. 22, **On Lieutenant Eyre's Narrative of the Disasters of Cabul**, p.35, **Conveyancing**, p. 52, **The Song of the Shirt**, p.54) 1799–1845. Most famous for his pun-filled humorous poems, but also wrote reflective and satirical poetry. Faced long struggles against poverty and illness with courage and good humour.

Gerard Manley Hopkins (**Spring and Fall**, p.25, **Binsey Poplars**, p.50) 1844–89. English poet and Catholic priest. Highly original in rhythms and in wordplay, his poems were ahead of their time and none were published during his lifetime. Became Professor of Greek at Dublin University in 1884.

A. E. Housman (**Into my heart...** , p.24, **On the Idle Hill**, p.43, **On Wenlock Edge**, p.49) 1859–1936. Alfred Edward Housman is best known for his collection of poems called *A Shropshire Lad*. His poetry is often rooted in his country background and is often melancholy in its awareness of time and passing youth. A classical scholar, he was appointed Professor of Latin at Cambridge in 1911.

John Keats (**To Autumn**, p.47) 1795–1821. English Romantic poet. His series of Odes, full of rich imagery and passionate feelings, are regarded as the finest ever written. The early death of his parents and brother, his experiences as a medical student, his frustrated love for Fanny Brawne and his own ill-health, made him sharply aware of the brevity of life and joy. Died aged 25.

Rudyard Kipling (**The Hyaenas**, p.41, **The Way Through the Woods**, p.49) 1865–1936. English novelist, poet and story-writer, very popular during his lifetime but criticised for his glorification of British imperialism since. His poem **If** remains one of the most popular ever written and he is remembered for stories as diverse as *The Jungle Book* and *The Man Who Would Be King*.

Amy Levy (**In the Mile End Road**, p.19) 1861–89. Born in Clapham to a Jewish family, Levy graduated from Cambridge and became well known as a feminist poet and novelist. Torn between her conventional upbringing and a more bohemian, literary lifestyle, and exhausted by publishing three novels in 1888, she committed suicide aged 27.

Richard Lovelace (**To Lucasta, Going to the Wars**, p.34) 1618–58. Cavalier poet and heroic defender of Charles I. Imprisoned twice during the Civil War. Died in poverty in the London slums.

Christopher Marlowe (**The Passionate Shepherd to His Love**, p.46). 1564–93. Considered the greatest Elizabethan playwright after Shakespeare (for *Dr Faustus*, *The Jew of Malta*, etc.). Lived a reckless and unconventional life, and was killed in a tavern brawl. His poetry is admired for its lyrical, pastoral beauty.

Andrew Marvell (**To His Coy Mistress**, p.9) 1621–78. Travelled widely. Elected to Parliament. Best known for his early love poetry and grouped with the *metaphysical* poets. Admired for the balanced and argumentative style of his writing.

Alice Meynell (**A Dead Harvest In Kensington Gardens**, p.53) 1847–1922. Born Alice Thompson. English poet and essayist. Converted to Catholicism. Many of her poems deal with the theme of religious mystery. Married author and editor, Wilfred Meynell, in 1877.

Henry Newbolt, Sir (**Vitaï Lampada**, p.35) 1862–1939. Best-known for his hearty, patriotic war poems. Also wrote on naval history and was appointed official Naval Historian in 1923.

Edith Nesbit (**The Gray Folk**, p.31 **Spring in War-Time**, p.111) 1858–1924. Novelist and poet. Founded the Fabian Society with her husband Hubert Bland and spread her radical political beliefs through writing and lecturing. Best-known for her books for children (especially *The Railway Children*). Wrote 44 novels.

Laetitia Pilkington (**A Song**, p.28). 1712–50. The first biographer of Jonathan Swift, she was divorced, imprisoned for debt and later scandalised eighteenth-century London with the details of her unconventional life.

Sir Walter Ralegh (**The Nymph's Reply to the Shepherd**, p.46) 1554–1618. Courtier, poet and adventurer, famous for introducing tobacco and potatoes to England, and for courteously spreading his cloak over a puddle for Elizabeth I. Executed for treason in the reign of James I.

Christina Rossetti (**Remember**, p.19, **The World**, p.56) 1830–93. English poet of Italian parentage. Admired for her religious lyrics and for the symbolism, vivid detail and intensity of feeling in her poetry. She was left an invalid and recluse by serious illness in 1874. Sister of poet and painter, Dante Gabriel Rossetti.

John Scott (**The Drum**, p.43) 1730–83. A devout Quaker and friend of Dr Johnson, Scott was a rich man who championed the poor and was outspoken in his criticism of evil and tyranny.

Anna Seward (**Verse Inviting Mrs. C – to Tea on a public Fast-day During the American War**, p.44) 1747–1809. Poet known as 'the swan of Lichfield'. Lived in the family home and cared for her ailing father. Expressed unconventional ideas such as hostility to marriage. Her poems were published by Sir Walter Scott.

William Shakespeare (**Sonnet 138**, p.11) 1564–1616. Shakespeare's 37 plays have made him the most famous and admired writer of all time, but he also found time to compose a series of 154 sonnets, many of which were addressed to a fascinating tormentor, known only as the 'Dark Lady'. The English or Shakespearian sonnet was eventually named after him because he was the greatest writer to use this form.

Percy Bysshe Shelley (**Ozymandias**, p.24) 1792–1822. Romantic poet who rejected conventional restraints on love and freedom and chose to live abroad with his second wife, Mary (the author of *Frankenstein*) because of ill-health, debt and criticisms of his lifestyle. A friend to both Byron and Keats, he drowned tragically young when his sailing boat was caught in a storm.

James Shirley (**Death the Leveller**, p.32) 1596–1666. Dramatist and poet. Studied at both Oxford and Cambridge. Converted to Catholicism. Became a schoolmaster and a very successful playwright. Fought on the Royalist side in the Civil War.

Robert Southey (**After Blenheim**, p.38) 1774–1843. Poet Laureate from 1813–43. One of the romantic 'Lake Poets' but not as well known as his friend, Coleridge. Wrote some admired biographies, including one about Lord Nelson.

Alfred, Lord Tennyson (**The Charge of the Light Brigade**, p.36, **The Eagle**, p.48) 1809–92. Succeeded Wordsworth as Poet Laureate in 1850. Very popular during the Victorian era but often criticised by twentieth-century writers for the sentimentality and narrow patriotism of his later work.

Walt Whitman (**Come up from the fields father**, p.39) 1819–92. American poet. *Leaves of Grass,* first published in 1855, was strikingly original and hugely influential in its directness and unorthodox rhythms. Deeply affected by nursing his wounded brother during the Civil War, he stayed on to work as a volunteer nurse in army hospitals.

Oscar Wilde (**Symphony in Yellow**, p.51) 1854–1900. Irish poet, dramatist and novelist, famous for his wit. He achieved great theatrical success in London for his comedies in the early 1890s. He was persecuted and imprisoned for his homosexuality in 1895, and died in Paris three years after his release.

William Wordsworth (**Composed Upon Westminster Bridge**, p.53) 1770–1850. Born in the Lake District, Wordsworth is the Romantic poet most concerned with the relationship between people and nature. He described himself as a 'worshipper of nature' and strove to convey nature's emotional impact. He succeeded Southey as Poet Laureate in 1843.

Thomas Wyatt, Sir (**They flee from me...**, p.16) 1503–42. A high-ranking member of Henry VIII's court, Ambassador to Spain and Commander of the Fleet. His translations of the Italian poet, Petrarch, introduced the sonnet form to England. Often praised for the honesty and strength of feeling in his poetry and compared to John Donne.

W. B. Yeats (The Lake Isle of Innisfree, p.51) 1865–1939. Irish poet and dramatist. His early poetry displays a romantic affection for pastoral Ireland. He founded the celebrated Abbey Theatre in Dublin and was a central figure in Irish artistic and political life. His later poems with their complex symbolism, Irish themes and great beauty are thought to be some of the greatest of the twentieth century. He was awarded the Nobel Prize for Literature in 1923.

(Post-1914)

Dannie Abse (Imitations, p.70) 1923– . Born into a Jewish family in Cardiff. Had two brothers who also achieved fame – one as a Labour MP and one as a psychoanalyst. Combined career as a doctor with writing poems, novels and plays until his retirement from medicine in 1982. Has published 15 collections of poetry. Married with children.

Fleur Adcock (Things, p.95) 1934– . Born in New Zealand. Much travelled in childhood. Settled in England in 1963. Her poems are often praised for their wit and individuality.

Simon Armitage (Poem, p.68) 1963– . Yorkshire-born poet. Qualified as a social worker and spent six years in the probation service. Has worked as a DJ and also writes song lyrics, plays and TV and radio scripts. Now a freelance writer and broadcaster.

Vera Brittain (Perhaps–, p.111) 1893–1970. Writer, pacifist and feminist. Her popular autobiographical work, *Testament of Youth*, describes her war-time experiences and struggle for education.

Thomas Burke (Of the Great White War, p.79) 1887–1945. British poet, novelist and travel writer. Known for stories and poems about the poor areas of London's East End. Some stories featured in *Alfred Hitchcock Presents* and *The Oxford Book of Twentieth Century Ghost Stories*.

Gillian Clarke (Baby-sitting, p.60, **Clocks**, p.72) 1937– . Welsh poet, playwright and translator. Teaches creative writing from primary school to university level. Has travelled widely to lecture and give readings. Her writing has been translated into ten languages. Lives on a smallholding in west Wales. Married with three children.

Margaret Postgate Cole (The Falling Leaves, p.108) 1893–1980. Poet, novelist and writer on economics and politics. Her brother and her husband (George Cole, socialist writer and historian) were conscientious objectors in the First World War. Known for the 30 detective novels she wrote with her husband.

Wendy Cope (Engineers' Corner, p.99) 1945– . Highly popular English poet. Taught in London primary schools after graduating from Oxford. Best known for her humorous poems and parodies of other writers.

Carol Ann Duffy (In Your Mind, p.92) 1955– . Born in Glasgow. Studied Philosophy at Liverpool University. Lives in Manchester where she teaches creative writing. Frequent poetry prize-winner including the Whitbread Award for *Mean Time*. Widely acclaimed as the leading female poet writing in Britain today.

Douglas Dunn (I Am a Cameraman, p.98) 1942– . Born in Scotland. Worked with Philip Larkin at Hull University Library. Became a Professor of English at St Andrews University. Won the Whitbread Prize for *Elegies* (1985).

Steve Ellis (To Edwin, at Eight Months, p.61, **West Pathway**, p.74) 1952– . Born in York. Professor of English Literature at the

University of Birmingham. Has published books about Chaucer, T. S. Eliot and a range of other poets, and three collections of his own poetry. Edwin is the elder of his two sons.

U. A. Fanthorpe (Growing Up, p.62) 1929– . A teacher and eventually Head of English at Cheltenham Ladies' College, Ursula Askham Fanthorpe has published seven collections of poetry in the last 20 years. She is a fellow of the Royal Society of Literature and was awarded a CBE for services to poetry in 2001.

Eleanor Farjeon (Easter Monday, p.85) 1881–1965. Daughter of a British novelist. Became famous as a writer of children's stories and songs. Awarded the Hans Christian Andersen Medal in 1958. Loved Edward Thomas and dedicated **Easter Monday** to him.

W. W. Gibson (Breakfast, p.83) 1878–1962. Wilfred Gibson received no formal education but was a social worker in London and an established poet before the war. Served in the ranks from 1914 but was not involved in front line action. Wrote with great sympathy about the experience of the ordinary soldier.

Ivor Gurney (The Target, p.103, **The Bohemians**, p.106) 1890–1937. Poet and composer. Was wounded and gassed on the Western Front. Committed to a mental institution in 1922 and spent the rest of his life in care.

Tony Harrison (from Long Distance, p.71) 1937– . Born in Leeds, the son of a baker. Won a scholarship and went on to teach at universities in Africa and Prague. Now recognised as Britain's leading film and theatre poet, writing for the National Theatre, the New York Metropolitan Opera, film and TV.

Seamus Heaney (Follower, p.69) 1939– . Born into a hard-working farming family in County Derry, Northern Ireland. Won a scholarship aged 12 and went on to teach after graduating from Queen's University, Belfast. Became one of Britain's most-admired poets and won the Nobel prize for Literature in 1995. Now lives in Dublin. Married with three children.

Agnes Grozier Herbertson (The Seed Merchant's Son, p.109) Dates unknown. Born in Oslo. Lived in Cornwall. Published books about medieval and heroic legends, and was a prolific author of children's books through the 1920s and 1930s.

Selima Hill (The Flowers, p.72, **The Hare**, p.96) 1945– . Worked as a tutor in hospitals and prisons and as a child-minder. Her father was a painter and writer. Her most recent collection of poems, *Bunny*, won the Whitbread Poetry Award for 2001.

Katherine Tynan Hinkson (Joining the Colours, p.103) 1861–1931. Dublin-born poet and novelist. A close friend of W. B. Yeats and part of the literary and theatrical revival in Dublin.

Ted Hughes (A Short Film, p.67) 1930–98. Yorkshire-born. Became one of Britain's best-known poets and Poet Laureate from 1984. Greatly admired for the energy and force of his writing. Married to Sylvia Plath until her death in 1963.

Anna Gordon Keown (Reported Missing, p.112) 1902–57. Novelist and poet. Married to writer and physician, Dr Philip Gosse.

Philip Larkin (I Remember, I Remember, p.65, **Wedding Wind**, p.93) 1922–85. Coventry-born poet and novelist who worked for many years as Hull University librarian. Regarded by many as the best English poet of his generation and admired for the honesty and precise control of his poetry.

Winifred M. Letts (The Deserter, p.107) 1887–1972. Irish poet, novelist and playwright. Wrote for the Abbey Theatre, Dublin. Married and moved to Kent where she spent the rest of her life.

Christopher Logue (Rat, O Rat..., p.91) 1926– . Born in Hampshire.

Poet, playwright, actor, translator and regular contributor to *Private Eye*.

E. A. Mackintosh (Recruiting, p.102) 1893–1917. Oxford-educated poet. Was wounded and gassed at the Somme and awarded the Military Cross. Became engaged while recovering in England. Killed at Cambrai in October 1917.

Florence Ripley Mastin (At the Movies, p.77) b. 1896. American writer and teacher of English and creative writing in New York. Her poem was first published in an American collection entitled *A Treasury of War Poetry* in 1919.

John McCrae (In Flanders Fields, p.108) 1872–1918. Canadian doctor who enlisted as a gunner. Transferred to the medical corps and was much admired for his medical work under fire. Wrote **In Flanders Fields** during the second Battle of Ypres and it became the most famous war poem of the time. Died of pneumonia in 1918.

Roger McGough (Defying Gravity, p.97) 1937– . Liverpool-born. One of Britain's best-known and most popular poets, famed for his live performances. Found success with the Liverpool poets and with the pop group, The Scaffold, and scripted the Beatles' film *Yellow Submarine*. Awarded the OBE in 1997.

Edna St Vincent Millay (Sonnet, p.81) 1892–1950. American poet. Reputation as a recklessly free spirit whose poetry celebrated love and moral freedom. Won the Pulitzer Prize in 1923. Especially noted for her sonnets.

Paul Muldoon (Anseo, p.66) 1951– . A poet inspired by his childhood in rural Northern Ireland, and by the Troubles. Worked for the BBC and later became a teacher of English and Creative Writing, and the Oxford Professor of Poetry. Lives and teaches in America, with his wife and two children.

Norman Nicholson (The Tune the Old Cow Died Of, p.73) 1914–87. A poet, novelist, playwright and reviewer strongly associated with Cumbria and the small mining community of Millom where he lived nearly all of his life. His poems often deal with the local people, the close-knit families and their struggles against poverty.

Wilfred Owen (Disabled, p.80, **Exposure**, p.82, **Mental Cases**, p.84, **The Send-Off**, p. 84, **Spring Offensive**, p.105, **The Parable of the Old Man and the Young**, p.110) 1893–1918. The best-known and most admired of all the First World War poets. Encouraged in his writing by Sassoon when they met in military hospital in 1917 after the Battle of the Somme. Awarded the Military Cross for exceptional bravery. Killed by machine-gun fire a week before the Armistice in November 1918.

Don Paterson (Bedfellows, p.96) 1963– . Born in Dundee. A poet, playwright and a jazz guitarist with five albums to his name. Won the prestigious T. S. Eliot Poetry Prize. Reviews computer games for *The Times*.

Sylvia Plath (You're, p.60, **Mirror**, p.95) 1932–63. American-born poet and novelist. Best known for the strikingly original and often disturbing imagery in her poetry. Committed suicide in London, one month after the publication of her only novel, *The Bell Jar*. Married to Ted Hughes, they had two children.

Jessie Pope (War Girls, p.78) 1868–1941. Published jauntily patriotic war poems in the *Daily Mail* and *Daily Express*, encouraging young men to enlist. Wilfred Owen's first draft of **Dulce et Decorum Est** was dedicated to her, suggesting that she was the 'friend' he denounces for glorifying the war.

Peter Porter (A Consumer's Report, p.88, **Mort aux Chats**, p.90) 1929– . Australian-born poet who has published over 20 poetry collections. Best known for his witty satires of western commercial society, often written in monologue form. Won the Whitbread prize in 1988.

Sheenagh Pugh (Sometimes, p.100) 1950– . Welsh-born poet, novelist and translator. Teaches creative writing at the University of Glamorgan. **Sometimes** has been used as an uplifting poem in a variety of contexts, including the Irish peace negotiations.

Henry Reed (Judging Distance, p.94) 1914–86. Poet, translator and dramatist. Wrote many radio plays in the 1950s but best known for his satirical treatment of army bureaucracy in his poems.

Isaac Rosenberg (Returning, We Hear the Larks, p.83) 1890–1918. Poet and artist from a poor urban Jewish background. Enlisted despite his weak chest and fought in the trenches on the Western Front. Killed in action in April 1918. Regarded by some as the best of the war poets after Owen.

Siegfried Sassoon (Base Details, p.79, **The Dug-Out**, p.81, **Lamentations**, p.106, **The Hero**, p.107) 1886–1967. Nicknamed 'Mad Jack' in the trenches because of his reckless courage, he won the Military Cross and was a hero to younger poets because of his forthright condemnation of the war.

Stevie Smith (To Carry the Child, p.64, **Oh Grateful Colours, Bright Looks!**, p.89) 1902–71. A poet and novelist, born in Hull, who lived for many years with an aged aunt. Became well known late in life for the originality and eccentricity of her poetry, and for her hugely popular public readings. Awarded the Queen's Gold Medal for poetry in 1969.

C. H. Sorley ('When you see millions of the mouthless dead...', p.77) 1895–1915. Charles Hamilton Sorley was born in Aberdeen, enlisted in 1914, became Captain and was killed in action at Loos in 1915. He left only 37 complete poems.

Sara Teasdale (There will come soft rains..., p.85) 1884–1933. American poet well known for the intensity of feeling in her poetry. Won a Pulitzer Prize for *Love Songs* in 1917. Became more and more withdrawn and eventually committed suicide. American science-fiction writer Ray Bradbury used the title (*There will come soft rains...*) for one of his short stories.

Lesbia Thanet (In Time of War, p.78) Dates unknown. Little is known about Thanet. Her poem was first published in a collection called *War Verse* in America during 1919.

Edward Thomas (As the Team's Head-Brass, p.76) 1878–1917. Oxford-educated poet. A friend of poets Robert Frost and Rupert Brooke. Well-known and admired for his nature poems. Killed in action at Arras, Easter 1917.

R. S. Thomas (The Cat and the Sea, p.89) 1913–2000. Ronald Stuart Thomas was a Welsh-born clergyman. His poetry is deeply concerned with the people and countryside of the remote Welsh parishes in which he worked.

Glossary

REFERENCE

allegory: a symbolic tale which often conveys a lesson or moral, as in **A Poison Tree** (p.30) or the **Ode** (p.42) or Nadine Gordimer's story, **The Train from Rhodesia**. See **symbolism**.

alliteration: the repetition of sounds at the beginning of words – usually two or more words in close proximity, as in 'blast-beruffled plume' in **The Darkling Thrush** (p.27). See **sound effects**.

allusion: a reference to something beyond the text which is designed to affect and to be understood by the reader, like the reference to 'Daimlers' to represent expensive cars in **Engineers' Corner** (p.99) or the references to unfashionable football teams to suggest the interests of the ordinary blokes in the trenches in **Breakfast** (p.83).

analogy: a comparison or example designed to emphasise similarities. Drayton makes the loss of love seem like the loss of life by using a death-bed analogy in **Since there's no help** (p.16).

antonym: a word that means the opposite of another word. In Faithless Sally Brown (p. 30) Hood uses opposites throughout his poem, e.g. 'Faint away' and 'brought to'; 'Tender ships' and 'hard-ship'; 'mermaid' and 'cannot swim'.

antithesis: the deliberate contrasting of opposed pairs. Simon Armitage uses an antithetical structure for effect throughout **Poem** (p.68) especially in the balanced final line, and Thomas Hood draws attention to his final pun by opposing '*Khans*' and 'can'ts' in the final two lines of **On Lieutenant Eyre's Narrative...** (p.35). See **contrast**.

assonance: repetition of the same vowel sound followed by different consonant sounds. Hardy uses assonance to link the two elements in his simile, 'bine-stems' and 'lyres' in **The Darkling Thrush** (p.27). The repetition of the same vowel *and* consonant sounds produces **rhyme** (like 'bine' and 'line', or 'lyre' and 'fire'). Armitage uses a mixture of assonance ('drive...side... night') which some people call 'weak rhyme' and strong rhyme ('lied' and 'side') in **Poem** (p.68). See **sound effects** and **simile**.

audience: the person or persons to whom the text is addressed, like the nymph in **The Passionate Shepherd** or the shepherd in **The Nymph's Reply** (p.46). Links with **narrator**, **point of view**.

ballad: a poetic form, usually of simple four-line stanzas and often telling a story, as in **The Ruined Maid** (p.10), **Faithless Sally Brown** (p.14).

caesura: a pause or stop for effect within a line of poetry, as in **Westminster Bridge** (p.53) after 'morning' in line 5, or in the final line of **Poem** (p.68).

characterisation: the ways in which a writer presents a character to the reader – though dialogue, direct description, contrast with other characters.

chronological: arranged according to the order of time - in date order.

cliche: an expression that has become 'worn out' or meaningless from being used too often. In The Unequal Fetters (p.12) the cliche 'time flies' appears as 'time that's flying'.

colloquialism: colloquial language is the language of everyday speech and often includes slang. Expressions like 'show their grit' and 'keep their end up' in **War Girls** (p.78) are colloquial. See **dialect**, **dialogue**.

compound word: two words linked together to create a new word, e.g. 'wind-wandering' or 'After-comers' in Binsey Poplars (p. 50). Hopkins uses many compound words - often words he has made up himself - throughout his poetry to create vivid images.

consonance: the repetition of consonant sounds, not just at the start of words (as in **alliteration**). In **The Darkling Thrush** (p.27) Thomas Hardy links 'corpse', 'crypt' and 'canopy' not only with the alliteration (based on the hard 'c' sound) but also with the consonance of the repeated 'p' sound. See **sound effects**.

contrast: the placing together of dissimilar things to emphasise their differences. Story-writers often contrast characters (like Chinua Achebe's headmaster and village priest in **Dead Men's Path**) and poets also use contrasting settings, moods, ideas. Philip Larkin contrasts his disappointing memories of growing up in Coventry with romanticised images of growing up in **I Remember, I Remember** (p.65). See **antithesis**.

couplet: two lines of poetry, paired together often by rhyme. Andrew Marvell writes **To His Coy Mistress** in rhyming couplets. Shakespeare concludes his sonnet (p.11) with a rhyming couplet, and rhyming couplets such as this, which use the iambic pentameter rhythm, are often called heroic couplets. See **rhythm**, **iambic pentameter**, **metre**, **sonnet**.

dialect: a regional and usually spoken form of language which differs from standard English and is often associated with a regional accent. One of Hardy's speakers in **The Ruined Maid** (p.10) uses the dialect word 'barton' (meaning 'farmyard') and refers to other dialect forms like 'thee' and 'thou'. William Barnes suggests a Dorset accent throughout **Woak Hill** (p.26) with his unconventional spelling ('voot-vall' for 'footfall', etc.).

dialogue: the words spoken by characters in stories or poems, in the form of **direct speech** – as if the writer is quoting them. Hardy's **The Ruined Maid** (p.10) takes the form of a conversation between two speakers and therefore consists entirely of dialogue or direct speech.

direct speech: see dialogue.

dramatic monologue: a poem in the form of a speaker addressing an unseen/unheard audience, as in **The Man He Killed** by Thomas Hardy. Hardy adopts the persona of an infantryman who has killed an enemy in battle. See **persona**, **narrator**, **point of view**.

enjambment: the running-on from one line of poetry to the next without pause. Enjambment is more worthy of comment when lines are run on across stanza breaks, as in Seamus Heaney's **Follower** (p.69) between stanzas II and III.

exclamation: an abrupt, loud or heightened utterance, often indicated by an exclamation mark (!). The words of Ozymandias are exclaimed in Shelley's poem on p.24, for instance.

euphemism: the use of a mild, inoffensive expression for something which is unpleasant or embarrassing. Death is a common subject for euphemism, as seen in Roger McGough's poem Defying Gravity (p.97).

fable: a legend or story that usually has a moral lesson. Often in old-fashioned fables writers would use animals that speak and act like human beings, e.g. in some of Chaucer's stories or in fairy-tales.

figurative language: the broad term for all 'figures of speech' (like simile, metaphor, personification) which go beyond literal meanings. Dannie Abse uses a figure of speech (personification) when he writes that 'snowflakes whitewash the shed roof and the grass' in **Imitations** (p.70). Obviously snowflakes are not people who can wield pots of whitewash and brushes, so this makes no literal sense, but it is packed with figurative meaning. See **metaphor**, **simile**, **personification**.

form: the type, pattern, shape or layout of a poem. See **structure**, **sonnet**, **ballad**, **lyric**, **narrative**, **dramatic monologue**, **couplet**, **enjambment**, **caesura**, **metre**, **iambic pentameter**, **repetition**, **sound effects**, **rhythm**, **rhyme**, **stanza**, **octave**, **sestet**, **quatrain**.

genre: a type of literature – like the short story or love poetry.

half-rhyme: a technique used in poetry in which the words do not quite rhyme, for example, in assonance. Don Paterson makes use of half-rhyme in **Bedfellows** (p.96), e.g. 'rest'/'wrist' and 'innuendo'/'window'. See **assonance**.

iambic pentameter: a rhythm in a line of poetry which has five weakly stressed syllables each followed by five strongly stressed syllables – in a 'de-dum de-dum de dum de dum de dum' pattern. The third stanza of Tony Harrison's **Long Distance** (p.71) has lines of regular iambic pentameter, but this rhythm breaks down in the final stanza. Regular patterns of rhythm in poetry are often called **metre**. See **rhythm**, **sonnet**.

imagery: images used by writers in which a picture, feeling or sense-impression is conveyed in words. Keats' **To Autumn** (p.47), for instance, is packed with images associated with this season and appeals to all the senses.

imperative: an order, instruction or command. Christina Rossetti issues instructions like 'Remember me' and 'do not grieve' in **Remember** (p.19).

irony: irony occurs when there is a difference between what is expected and what actually happens, as in the ironic twists at the end of several of the **Opening Worlds** stories or in poems such as **Disabled** (p.80) where Owen reveals that the now legless soldier was once an admired footballer. Irony also refers to the use of implied meanings which are often the direct opposite of what is stated. For instance, Wendy Cope is being ironic throughout **Engineers' Corner** (p.99) 'small boys dream of writing couplets / And spurn the bike, the lorry and the train'.

juxtaposition: the placing together of words and ideas for a particular effect. See **antithesis**, **contrast**.

lyric: originally a poem which was meant to be sung, but *lyrical* poetry now suggests a short poem which expresses feelings (especially love) rather than telling a story, as in Robert Herrick's **Upon Julia's Clothes** (p.8).

metaphysical poetry: poems produced by John Donne and other sixteenth- and seventeenth-century poets which are famous for extended and often highly original metaphors and striking images. Donne's metaphorical conversation with the sun is extended throughout **The Sun Rising** (p.8) for instance.

metaphor: an image which describes one thing in terms of a very different thing but without making the link as obvious as in a simile. Gillian Clarke describes 'the perfume/Of her breath' and suggests metaphorically that the baby's breath is sweet and fragrant in **Baby-sitting** (p.60). If she had written that the baby's breath was 'like perfume', it would have been a simile. A metaphor becomes **extended** when the links are developed beyond one reference. For instance, Roger McGough describes the death of his rugby-playing friend (and his release from his illness) using several metaphors taken from rugby in **Defying Gravity** (p.97) – 'tackle . . . sidestep . . . wing . . .' See **simile**, **figurative language**, **personification**, **metaphysical poetry**.

metre: see **iambic pentameter** and **rhythm**.

mock-heroic: a way of writing in which the poet adopts a heroic style for satirical effect, usually on a very unheroic subject. Anna Seward uses highly poetic language to create humour by satirising an invitation to tea in **Verses Inviting. . .** (p.78). See **satire**.

mood: the atmosphere and feelings suggested, like patriotic pride and optimism in **War Girls** or the anxiety and vulnerability in **In Time of War** (p.78). See **tone**.

narrative: a story – so narrative poetry is poetry which tells a story, like **The Charge of the Light Brigade** (p.36).

narrator: the person or voice telling the story. This can be very different from the voice of the writer. In **Wedding-Wind** (p.93), Philip Larkin uses a recently married woman as his narrator and writes the whole poem from her point of view. This kind of narrator is often called a **persona** when the voice and character are different from the writer's. See **point of view**.

octave: a group of eight lines of poetry. See **sonnet**.

ode: a poem of celebration, originally dedicated to an individual or marking a particular event, but now a more personal expression of admiration or wonder, as in Keats' **To Autumn** (p.47).

onomatopoeia: occurs when the sound of a word echoes or suggests its meaning. There are very few genuine examples of sound-words (like 'buzz', 'miaow', 'hiss') in the language. Tennyson may be describing sounds in **The Charge of the Light Brigade** (p.36) 'Cannon . . . Volleyed and thundered' but he's not really using onomatopoeia. It's safer to point out 'onomatopoeic effect' in words like 'twitter' (the sound of the swallows at the end of **To Autumn**, p.47) or 'breathless hush' (the 'shushing' sound in **Vitaï Lampada**, p.35) than it is to claim that you can see onomatopoeia everywhere. See **sound effects**, **plosive sounds**, **sibilant sounds**.

oxymoron: a contradiction in terms, placed very close to each other, like 'grimly gay' in Wilfred Owen's **The Send-Off** (p.104). See **antithesis**, **contrast**.

parody: an imitation of another work, designed to amuse. Sir Walter Ralegh parodies Christpher Marlowe's **Passionate Shepherd . . .** in **The Nymph's Reply . . .** (p.46). Peter Porter parodies a political speech designed to whip up hatred and prejudice in **Mort aux Chats** (p.90).

pathos: used in prose or poetry where the writer provokes feelings of sadness, pity or sympathy in the reader. Pathos is a technique used in many of the stories in Opening Worlds, for instance in **The Tall Woman . . .**, **The Train**

from **Rhodesia**, and **The Pieces of Silver**, amongst others.

pastoral: originally referred to a story or poem which was about shepherds, but now covers any attractive description of country life, as in **The Way Through the Woods** (p.49) or **The Lake Isle of Innisfree** (p.51).

pathetic fallacy: the presentation of nature, the weather, inanimate objects as if they have feelings – or to reflect the feelings of the writer or of characters. Philip Larkin uses the weather to suggest the feelings of the wife in **Wedding-Wind** (p.93). Thomas Hardy uses his description of the bleak landscape to reflect his 'fervourless' mood in **The Darkling Thrush** (p.27). See **personification**, **metaphor**.

persona: see **narrator**, **point of view**.

personification: a kind of metaphor where ideas, objects, elements of nature, are given human characteristics for effect, as in the opening of **The Sun Rising** (p.8) where Donne characterises the sun as a person who is 'Busy', 'unruly' and a 'fool'. See **figurative language**, **metaphor**, **simile**.

plosive sounds: consonant sounds which rely on the build-up and release of breath, like 'b' and 'p'. See **onomatopoeia**, **sound effects**.

point of view: the position adopted by the writer which can be changed for effect. For instance Tony Harrison gives us his father's point of view in the third stanza of **Long Distance** (p.71) and then gives us his own point of view in the final stanza. Siegfried Sassoon gives us the mother's view of her dead son as a hero in the first two stanzas of **The Hero** (p.107) and then contrasts this with the Officer's memory of the son in the final stanza. Marlowe adopts the point of view of a shepherd and Ralegh a nymph (p.46). See **narrator**, **persona**.

pun: a humorous play on similar-sounding words. Thomas Hood's poetry is packed with puns, as in the final stanza of **Faithless Sally Brown** (p.15), where he plays on the words 'told' (*informed*) and 'toll'd' (*rang*).

punctuation: the use of marks (full stops, commas, speech marks, dashes, question marks etc) to organise the words and show how they should be read. In **The Man He Killed** (p.42), Hardy uses dashes in stanza IV to suggest the casual way in which men decide to enlist in the army.

quatrain: a group of four lines of poetry. See **sonnet**.

repetition: writers, especially poets, often use repeated words, lines or whole structures for effect, as in Vera Brittain's use of 'perhaps' at the opening of each stanza (except the last one) of **Perhaps –** (p.111) or Hardy concluding each stanza of **The Ruined Maid** with the point of view of the maid herself and the words 'said she', almost like a chorus.

rhetoric: language designed to influence, persuade or move an audience – as in speech-making. There are elements of rhetoric in many poems. Wordsworth convincing us of the beauty of London in **Composed Upon Westminster Bridge** (p.53) or Peter Porter getting us to laugh at discrimination and prejudice by appearing to hate cats in **Mort aux Chats** (p.90).

rhetorical question: a question posed for effect, which requires no answer, as in the repeated question at the end of Wilfred Owen's **Disabled** (p.80). Any features of language (questions, orders, repetition, sound effects) which are used to influence or persuade an audience can be called **rhetorical devices**.

rhyme: see **assonance**. Regular patterns of rhyme at the end of lines are very common in poetry. Changes in these patterns or the linking of key words through rhyme are often the best features to look out for and comment on. Tony Harrison changes the pattern of the rhyme (or the **rhyme scheme**) in the final stanza of **Long Distance** (p.71) for instance. Siegfried Sassoon ends **Base Details** with the only couplet in the poem and links the words 'dead' and 'bed' through rhyme. Why do you think this is? See **rhythm, couplet, iambic pentameter, form**.

rhythm: patterns created by placing of words and the beats they create. You can probably hear the rhythm of marching in **The Drum** (p.43) with four strong (or stressed) beats in each line. Why do you think this is changed in the final line of each stanza to *five* stressed beats? If rhythm is absolutely regular, there's not much to say about it, but changes in rhythm (what Thomas Hardy called 'cunning irregularity') can be very significant. See **iambic pentameter**.

satire: a poem or story can be described as 'satirical' if it sets out to criticise and change human behaviour by using ridicule, as in **A Song** (p.28) where Laetitia Pilkington ridicules the dishonesty of lovers, politicians and clerics.

sestet: a group of six lines of poetry. See **sonnet**.

sibilant sounds: consonant sounds (especially 's' and 'z') which create a hissing sound, as in the opening line of **Exposure** (p.82) which has *seven* sibilant sounds. See **sound effects**.

simile: a comparison which brings together words and images from different areas for effect, usually using 'like' or 'as'. Hardy uses a simile when he writes that the 'tangled bine-stems' are 'Like strings of broken lyres' in **The Darkling Thrush** (p.27). See **metaphor**.

sonnet: a 14-line poem, usually a love poem and usually with a clear rhythmical (often iambic pentameter) and rhyming pattern. The Italian or Petrarchan sonnet is divided into an octave (eight-line section) and a sestet (six-line section), like **Composed Upon Westminster Bridge** (p.53). The English or Shakespearian sonnet is divided into three quatrains (four-line section) and a final couplet, like **Poem** (p.68) and there are variations on both of these forms to be found in **Opening Lines**. The pattern tends to reflect the poet's train of thought. See **iambic pentameter**.

sound effects: many writers, especially poets, exploit the sound and music of language, using repeated elements to produce rhythm, rhyme, alliteration, assonance, consonance – and particularly effective sounds: onomatopoeic, plosive, sibilant.

stanza: a group of lines into which poems are often divided, which is often called a 'verse' and marked out by a particular rhythmic or rhyming pattern. **Faithless Sally Brown** (p.14) has 17 stanzas.

structure: the pattern, shape, layout or organisation of a poem (or story). See **form**.

stylised: refers to language that follows a conventional style or pattern, rather than being natural, like everyday speech. Stevie Smith's language is more like a formal speech or sermon in **To Carry the Child** (p.64): 'Oh it is not happy,/ its is never happy . . . be guilty of no man's blood'.

symbolism: the use of one thing to represent another. Marvell's uses 'worms' in **To His Coy Mistress** (p.9) not only to symbolise decay in death, but also to suggest the male sexual organ. The 'deep drums' in **In Time of War** (p.78) symbolise the ominous call to arms. See **allegory**.

theme: what a poem or story is about, at a deeper level than the story. The subject/moral/lesson to be learned, so the theme of **Into My Heart** (p.24) might be the loss of childish innocence.

tone: the attitude of the writer conveyed in the *tone of voice*. The tone of **To His Coy Mistress** (p.9) might be described as impatient, argumentative, coaxing. The tone of the 'ruined maid' in the final stanza of Hardy's poem (p.10) might be described as smug, condescending, unashamed. See **mood**.

ACKNOWLEDGEMENTS

The Publishers gratefully acknowledge the following for permission to reproduce copyright material. Whilst every effort has been made to trace the copyright holders, in cases where this has proved unsuccessful or if any have inadvertently been overlooked, the Publishers will be pleased to make the necessary arrangements at the first opportunity.

Extracts from 'Into my heart an air that kills' and 'On Wenlock Edge' by A. E. Housman: reprinted by permission of The Society of Authors as the Literary Representative of The Estate of A. E. Housman. Extracts from 'The Lake Isle of Innisfree' by W. B. Yeats: reprinted by permission of A. P. Watt Limited on behalf of Michael B. Yeats. Extracts from 'The Hyaenas' and 'The Way Through The Wood's by Rudyard Kipling: reprinted by permission of A. P. Watt Limited on behalf of The National Trust for Places of Historical Interest or Natural Beauty. Extracts from 'Vitaï Lampada' by Henry Newbolt published in *Selected Poems of Henry Newbolt* by Hodder & Stoughton 1981: reprinted with the kind permission of Peter Newbolt. Extract from 'Poem' by Simon Armitage Copyright © Simon Armitage: reprinted by permission of David Godwin Associates. Extract from 'Baby Sitting' and 'Clocks' by Gillian Clarke from *Collected Poems* published by Carcanet Press Limited: reprinted with permission of Carcanet Press Limited. Extract from 'To Edwin' by Steve Ellis published in *West Pathway* by Bloodaxe Books 1993 Copyright © Steve Ellis 1993: reprinted with the kind permission of the author. Extract from 'Long Distance II' by Tony Harrison published in *Selected Poems* by Penguin Copyright © Tony Harrison: reprinted by permission of Gordon Dickerson on behalf of Tony Harrison. Extract from 'The Flowers' by Selima Hill from *Trembling Hearts in the Bodies of Dogs: New and Selected Poems* published by Bloodaxe Books 1994: reprinted by permission of Bloodaxe Books. Extract from 'The Tune The Old Cow Died Of' by Norman Nicholson from *Collected Poems* published by Faber and Faber Limited: reprinted by permission of David Higham Associates Limited. Extract from 'I Remember, I Remember' and 'Wedding Winds' by Philip Larkin first published in *Less Deceived* by Marvell Press, Australia © Philip Larkin: reprinted by permission of Marvell Press, England and Australia. Extracts from 'Follower' by Seamus Heaney from *Opened Ground* by Seamus Heaney published by Faber and Faber Limited: reprinted by permission of Faber and Faber Limited. Extract from 'A Short Film' by Ted Hughes from *Birthday Letters* by Ted Hughes published by Faber and Faber Limited: reprinted by permission of Faber and Faber Limited. Extract from 'Anseo' by Paul Muldoon from *New Selected Poems* by Paul Muldoon published by Faber and Faber Limited: reprinted by permission of Faber and Faber Limited. Four postcards from *http://info.ox.ac.uk/jtap*. Extract from 'I am a cameraman' by Douglass Dunn from *Selected Poems* by Douglas Dunn published by Faber and Faber Limited: reprinted by permission of Faber and Faber Limited. Extract from 'Bedfellows' by Don Paterson from *Nil Nil* by Don Paterson published by Faber and Faber Limited: reprinted by permission of Faber and Faber Limited. Extracts from 'You're' and 'Mirror' by Sylvia Plath from *Collected Poems* by Sylvia Plath published by Faber and Faber Limited: reprinted by permission of Faber and Faber Limited. Extract from 'Engineers Corner' by Wendy Cope from *Making Cocoa for Kingsley Amis* by Wendy Cope published by Faber and Faber Limited: reprinted by permission of Faber and Faber Limited. Extract from 'Rat O Rat' by Christopher Logue from *Selected Poems* by Christopher Logue published by Faber and Faber Limited: reprinted by permission of Faber and Faber Limited. Extract from 'Growing Up' by U. A. Fanthorpe from *Voices Off* published by Peterloo Poets 1984: reprinted with the kind permission of the author. Extract from 'To Carry The Child' by Stevie Smith: reprinted with the kind permission of The Estate of James MacGibbon. Extract from 'Easter Monday' by Eleanor Farjeon from *Book of Days* published by Oxford University Press: reprinted by permission of David Higham Associates Limited. Extract from 'Breakfast' by W. W. Gibson from Collected Poems published by Macmillan: reprinted by permission of the publishers. Extract 'Sonnet' by Edna St. Vincent Millay from *Collected Poems* published by Carcanet Press Limited: reprinted by permission of Carcanet Press Limited. Extracts from 'Base Details', 'The Hero' and 'The Dug-Out' by Siegfried Sassoon Copyright © Siegfried Sassoon: reprinted by kind permission of George Sassoon via Barbara Levy Literary Agency. Extract from 'There Will Come Soft Rains' by Sara Teasdale from *The Collected Poems of Sara Teasdale* published by Macmillan, New York 1937: reprinted with the permission of Simon & Schuster Inc. Extract from 'Defying Gravity' by Roger McGough from *Defying Gravity* published by Penguin Books Copyright © Roger McGough: reprinted by permission of Peters Fraser & Dunlop on behalf of Roger McGough. Extract from 'Judging Distances' by *Henry Reed, from Henry Reed: Collected Poems* edited by Jon Stallworthy published by Oxford University Press 1991: reprinted by permission of Oxford University Press. Extract from 'Sometimes' by Sheenagh Pugh, from Selected Poems Copyright © Sheenagh Pugh 1990 published by Seren Books: reprinted by permission of the publishers. Extract from 'Perhaps' by Vera Brittain is reprinted with the kind permission of her literary executors, Mark Bostridge and Rebecca Williams. Extract from 'The Target' by Ivor Gurney: reprinted by permission of the Ivor Gurney Trust. Extract from 'The Deserter' by Winifred Letts from *Hallowe'en and Poems of the War* published by John Murray: reprinted with permission of John Murray (Publishers) Limited. Extract from 'The Falling Leaves' by Margaret Cole: reprinted by permission of David Higham Associates Limited. Extract from 'Reported Missing' by Anna Gordon Keown. Extract from 'Dead Man's Path' by Chinua Achebe published by Heinemann Educational: reprinted by permission of REPP. Extract from 'Snapshots of a Wedding' by Bessie Head, published by Heinemann Educational: reprinted by permission of REPP. Extract from 'The Tall woman and her Short Husband' by Feng Ji-Cai translated to English by Gladys Yang © English Translation Gladys Young: reprinted by permission of Yang Zhi (daughter of Gladys Young). Extract from 'The Train to Rhodesia' by Nadine Gordimer from *Selected Stories* published by Jonathan Cape: reprinted by permission of A. P. Watt Limited on behalf of Nadine Gordimer. Extract from 'The Young Couple' by Ruth Prawer Jhabvala from *A Stronger Climate* published by John Murray (Publishers) Limited: reprinted by permission of the publishers. Extract from 'The Red Ball' by Ismith Khan from *A Day in the Country* by Ismith Khan published by Peepal Tree Press 1994: reprinted by permission of the publishers. Extract from *'Games at Twilight'* by Anita Desai from Games At Twilight first published by Vintage Copyright © Anita Desai 1978: reproduced by permission of Rogers Coleridge & White Limited, 20 Powis Mews, London W11 1JN. Extract from 'The Winter Oak' by Yuri Nagibin. 'Leela's Friend' by R. K. Narayan from *Malguidi Days* first published in Great Britain by William Heinemann in 1982 Copyright © 1972, 1975, 1978, 1980, 1981, 1982 by R. K. Narayan: reprinted by permission of Sheil Land Associates Limited. 'The Pieces of Silver' by Karl Sealy: reprinted by kind permission of Beryl Sealy wife of the late Karl Sealy. Extract from 'The Gold-Legged Frog' translated by Domern Garden from *The Politician and Other Stories* published by Silkworm Books: reprinted by permission of the author and Silkworm Books. Extract from 'Two Kinds' by Amy Tan from *The Joy Luck Club* © 1989 Amy Tan: reprinted by permission of Abner Stein.